THE ORIGIN AND NATURE

of the

EMOTIONS

THE ORIGIN AND NATURE

of the

EMOTIONS

Miscellaneous Papers

BY

GEORGE W. CRILE, M.D.

PROFESSOR OF SURGERY, SCHOOL OF MEDICINE, WESTERN RESERVE UNIVERSITY
VISITING SURGEON TO THE LAKESIDE HOSPITAL, CLEVELAND

EDITED BY

AMY F. ROWLAND, B. S.

McGrath Publishing Company

College Park, Maryland

1970

Reprinted by
McGrath Publishing Co., 1970

ISBN: 0-8434-0082-X
LC#73-119228

Reprinted from the copy at
Duke University Medical Center Library

Manufactured in the United States of America
by Arno Press, Inc., New York

PREFACE

IN response to numerous requests I have brought together into this volume eight papers which may serve as a supplement to the volumes previously published* and as a preface to monographs now in preparation.

In the first of these addresses, the Ether Day Address, delivered at the Massachusetts General Hospital in October, 1910, I first enunciated the Kinetic Theory of Shock, the key to which was found in laboratory researches and in a study of Darwin's "Expression of the Emotions in Man and in Animals," whereby the phylogenetic origin of the emotions was made manifest and the pathologic identity of surgical and emotional shock was established. Since 1910 my associates and I have continued our researches through— (a) Histologic studies of all the organs and tissues of the body; (b) Estimation of the H-ion concentration of the blood in the emotions of anger and fear and after the application of many other forms of stimuli; (c) Functional tests of the adrenals, and (d) Clinical observations.

It would seem that if the striking changes produced by fear and anger and by physical trauma in the master organ of the body—the brain—were due to *work*, then we should expect to find corresponding histologic changes in other organs of the body as well. We therefore examined every

* Surgical Shock, 1899; Surgery of the Respiratory System, 1899; Problems Relating to Surgical Operations, 1901; Blood Pressure in Surgery, 1903; Hemorrhage and Transfusion, 1909; Anemia and Resuscitation, 1914; and Anoci-association, 1914 (with Dr. W. E. Lower).

iii

organ and tissue of the bodies of animals which had been subjected to intense fear and anger and to infection and to the action of foreign proteins, some animals being killed immediately; some several hours after the immediate effects of the stimuli had passed; some after séances of strong emotion had been repeated several times during a week or longer.

The examination of all the tissues and organs of these animals showed changes in three organs only, and with few exceptions in all three of these organs—the brain, the adrenals, and the liver. The extent of these changes is well shown by the photomicrographs which illustrate the paper on "The Kinetic System" which is included in this volume. This paper describes many experiments which show that the brain, the adrenal, and the liver play together constantly and that no one of these organs—as far at least as is indicated by the histologic studies—can act without the co-operation of the other two.

Another striking fact which has been experimentally established is that the deterioration of these three organs caused by emotion, by exertion, and by other causes is largely counteracted, if not exclusively, during sleep. If animals exhausted by the continued application of a stimulus are allowed complete rest for a certain number of hours, *without sleep*, the characteristic histologic appearance of exhaustion in the brain, adrenals, and liver is not altered notably, whereas in animals allowed to sleep for the same number of hours the histologic changes in these organs are lessened—in some cases obliterated even.

This significant phenomenon and its relation will be dealt with in a later monograph.

Many of the arguments and illustrations by which the primary premises were established are repeated—a few in all—many in more than one of these addresses. It will be observed, however, that the *application* of these premises varies, and that their *significance* broadens progressively.

In the Ether Day Address the phylogenetic key supplied by Darwin was utilized to formulate the principle that the organism reacts as a unit to the stimuli of physical injury, of emotion, of infection, etc. To the study of these reactions (transformations of energy) the epoch-making work of Sherrington, "The Integrative Action of the Nervous System," gave an added key by which the dominating rôle of the brain was determined. Later the original work of Cannon on the adrenal glands gave facts, and an experimental method by which Darwin's phylogenetic theory of the emotions was further elaborated in other papers, especially in the one entitled "Phylogenetic Association in Relation to the Emotions," read before The American Philosophical Society in April, 1911.

GEORGE W. CRILE.

CLEVELAND, OHIO, *February, 1915.*

CONTENTS

THE ORIGIN AND NATURE OF THE EMOTIONS

PHYLOGENETIC ASSOCIATION IN RELATION TO CERTAIN MEDICAL PROBLEMS *

The discovery of the anesthetic properties of ether and its practical application to surgery must always stand as one of the great achievements of medicine. It is eminently fitting that the anniversary of that notable day, when the possibilities of ether were first made known to the world, should be celebrated within these walls, and whatever the topic of your Ether Day orator, he must fittingly pause first to pay tribute to that great event and to the master surgeons of the Massachusetts General Hospital. On this occasion, on behalf of the dumb animals as well as on behalf of suffering humanity, I express a deep sense of gratitude for the blessings of anesthesia.

Two years ago, an historic appreciation of the discovery of ether was presented here by Professor Welch, and last year an address on medical research was given by President Eliot. I, therefore, will not attempt a general address, but will invite your attention to an experimental and clinical study. In presenting the summaries of the large amount of data in these researches, I acknowledge with gratitude the

* Address delivered at the Massachusetts General Hospital on the sixty-fourth anniversary of Ether Day, Oct. 15, 1910.

1

great assistance rendered by my associates, Dr. D. H. Dolley, Dr. H. G. Sloan, Dr. J. B. Austin, and Dr. M. L. Menten.*

The scope of this paper may be explained by a concrete example. When a barefoot boy steps on a sharp stone there is an immediate discharge of nervous energy in his effort to escape from the wounding stone. This is not a voluntary act. It is not due to his own personal experience—his ontogeny—but is due to the experience of his progenitors during the vast periods of time required for the evolution of the species to which he belongs, i. e., his phylogeny. The wounding stone made an impression upon the nerve receptors in the foot similar to the innumerable injuries which gave origin to this nerve mechanism itself during the boy's vast phylogenetic or ancestral experience. The stone supplied the phylogenetic association, and the appropriate discharge of nervous energy automatically followed. If the sole of the foot be repeatedly bruised or crushed by a stone, shock may be produced; if the stone be only lightly applied, then the consequent sensation of tickling causes a discharge of nervous energy. In like manner there have been implanted in the body other mechanisms of ancestral or phylogenetic origin whose purpose is the discharge of nervous energy for the good of the individual. In this paper I shall discuss the origin and mode of action of some of these mechanisms and their relation to certain phases of anesthesia.

The word anesthesia—meaning *without feeling*—describes accurately the effect of ether in anesthetic dosage. Although no pain is felt in operations under inhalation anesthesia, the

* From the H. K. Cushing Laboratory of Experimental Medicine, Western Reserve University, Cleveland.

nerve impulses excited by a surgical operation still reach the brain. We know that not every portion of the brain is fully anesthetized, since surgical anesthesia does not kill. The question then is: What effect has trauma under surgical anesthesia upon the part of the brain *that remains awake?* If, in surgical anesthesia, the traumatic impulses cause an excitation of the wide-awake cells, are the remainder of the cells of the brain, despite anesthesia, affected in any way? If so, they are prevented by the anesthesia from expressing that influence in conscious perception or in muscular action. Whether the *anesthetized* cells are influenced or not must be determined by noting the physiologic functions of the body after anesthesia has worn off, and in animals by an examination of the brain-cells as well. It has long been known that the vasomotor, the cardiac, and the respiratory centers discharge energy in response to traumatic stimuli applied to various sensitive regions of the body during surgical anesthesia. If the trauma be sufficient, exhaustion of the entire brain will be observed after the effect of the anesthesia has worn off; that is to say, despite the complete paralysis of voluntary motion and the loss of consciousness due to ether, the traumatic impulses that are known to reach the *awake* centers in the medulla also reach and influence every other part of the brain. Whether or not the consequent functional depression and the morphologic alterations seen in the brain-cells may be due to the low blood-pressure which follows excessive trauma is shown by the following experiments: The circulation of animals was first rendered *static* by over-transfusion, and was controlled by a continuous blood-pressure record on a drum, the factor of anemia being thereby wholly excluded during the application of the trauma and during the removal of a specimen of brain tissue for histologic study. In each instance, morphologic changes in the cells of all parts of the brain were found, but it required much more trauma to produce brain-cell changes in animals whose blood-pressure was kept at the normal level than in the animals whose blood-pressure was allowed to take a downward course. In the cortex and in the cerebellum, the changes in the brain-cells were in every instance more marked than in the medulla.

There is also strong *negative* evidence that traumatic impulses are not excluded by ether anesthesia from the part of the brain that is apparently asleep. This evidence is as follows: If the factor of fear be excluded, and if in addition the traumatic impulses be prevented from reaching the brain by cocain* blocking, then, despite the intensity or the duration of the trauma within the zone so blocked, there follows no exhaustion after the effect of the anesthetic disappears, and no morphologic changes are noted in the brain-cells.

Still further negative evidence that inhalation anesthesia offers little or no protection to the brain-cells against trauma is derived from the following experiment: A dog whose spinal cord had been divided at the level of the first dorsal segment, and which had then been kept in good condition for two months, showed a recovery of the spinal reflexes, such as the scratch reflex, etc. Such an animal is known as a "spinal dog." Now, in this animal, the abdomen and hind extremities had no direct nerve connection with the brain. In this dog, continuous severe trauma of the abdominal viscera and of the hind extremities lasting for four

---

* Since the presentation of this paper, novocain has been substituted for cocain in operations under anoci-association.

FIG. 1.

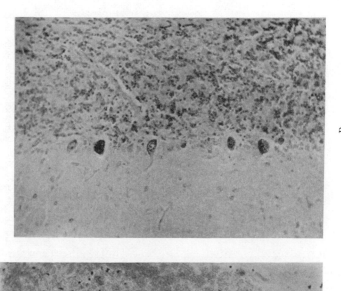

A

SECTION OF CEREBELLUM OF DOG—NORMAL (× 310).

B

SECTION OF CEREBELLUM OF A DOG WHICH RECEIVED SEVERE MANIPULATION OF THE ABDOMINAL VISCERA IN AN ATTEMPT TO CAUSE SHOCK, THE SPINAL CORD HAVING BEEN PREVIOUSLY SEVERED AT THE SEVENTH CERVICAL VERTEBRA (× 310).

Note the normal condition of the Purkinje cells in B, the shock-producing impulses having been prevented from reaching them by the division of the cord.

FIG. 2.

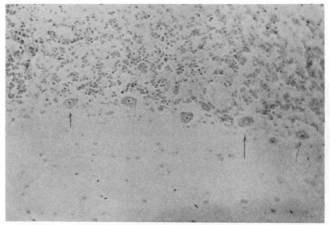

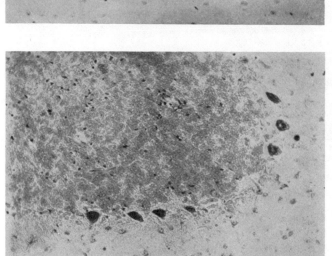

A

SECTION OF CEREBELLUM OF DOG—NORMAL (× 310).

B

SECTION OF CEREBELLUM OF A DOG AFTER PHYSICAL TRAUMA UNDER ETHER (× 310).

Note the absence of hyperchromatic cells in B and the signs of disintegration in the cells indicated by arrows.

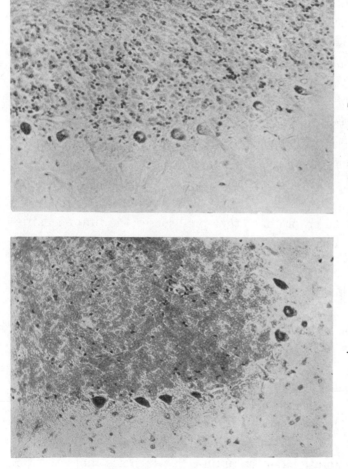

FIG. 3.

A

SECTION OF CEREBELLUM OF DOG—NORMAL (× 310).

B

SECTION OF CEREBELLUM OF A DOG AFTER PHYSICAL TRAUMA UNDER NITROUS OXID ANESTHESIA (× 310).

Note the protective effect of nitrous oxid by comparing B with the preceding photomicrograph of the brain-cells of the dog which received equal trauma under ether.

hours was accompanied by but slight change in either the circulation or in the respiration, and by no microscopic alteration of the brain-cells (Fig. 1). Judging from a large number of experiments on *normal* dogs under ether, such an amount of trauma would have caused not only complete physiologic exhaustion of the brain, but also morphologic alterations of all of the brain-cells and the physical destruction of many (Fig. 2). We must, therefore, conclude that, although ether anesthesia produces unconsciousness, it *apparently protects none of the brain-cells* against exhaustion from the trauma of surgical operations; ether is, so to speak, but a veneer. Under nitrous oxid anesthesia there is approximately only one-fourth as much exhaustion as is produced by equal trauma under ether (Fig. 3). We must conclude, therefore, either that nitrous oxid protects the brain-cells against trauma or that ether predisposes the brain-cells to exhaustion as a result of trauma. With these premises let us now inquire into the cause of this exhaustion of the brain-cells.

The Cause of the Exhaustion of the Brain-cells as a Result of Trauma of Various Parts of the Body under Inhalation Anesthesia

Numerous experiments on animals to determine the effect of ether anesthesia *per se, i. e.*, ether anesthesia without trauma, showed that, although certain changes were produced, these included neither the physiologic exhaustion nor the alterations in the brain-cells which are characteristic of the effects of trauma. On turning to the study of trauma, we at once found in the behavior of individuals as a whole under deep and under light anesthesia the clue to the cause of the discharge of energy, of the consequent physiologic exhaustion, and of the morphologic changes in the brain-cells.

If, in the course of abdominal operations, rough manipulations of the parietal peritoneum be made, there will be frequently observed a marked increase in the respiratory rate and an increase in the expiratory force which may be marked by the production of an audible expiratory groan. Under light ether anesthesia, severe manipulations of the peritoneum often cause such vigorous contractions of the abdominal muscles that the operator is greatly hindered in his work.

Among the unconscious responses to trauma under ether anesthesia are purposeless moving, the withdrawal of the injured part, and, if the anesthesia be sufficiently light and the trauma sufficiently strong, there may be an effort toward escape from the injury. In injury under ether anesthesia every grade of response may be seen, from the slightest change in the respiration or in the blood-pressure to a vigorous defensive struggle. As to the purpose of these subconscious movements in response to injury, there can be no doubt—*they are efforts to escape from the injury.*

Picture what would be the result of a formidable abdominal operation extending over a period of half an hour or more on an unanesthetized human patient, during which extensive adhesions had been broken up, or a large tumor dislodged from its bed! In such a case, would not the nervous system discharge its energy to the utmost in efforts to escape from the injury, and would not the patient suffer complete exhaustion? If the traumata under inhalation anesthesia are sufficiently strong and are repeated in sufficient numbers, the brain-cells are finally deprived of their dischargeable nervous energy and become exhausted just as exhaustion follows such strenuous and prolonged muscular exertion as is seen in endurance tests.   Whether the energy

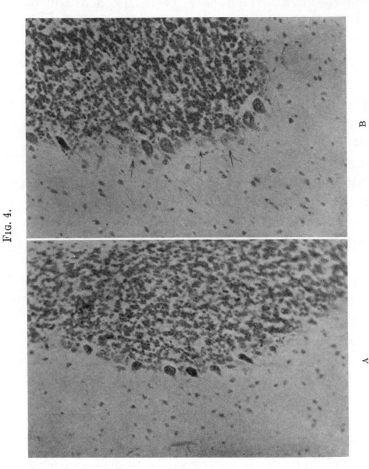

FIG. 4.

A

SECTION OF CEREBELLUM OF NORMAL FOX (× 310).

B

SECTION OF CEREBELLUM OF FOX EXHAUSTED BY A SEVEN-MILE CHASE (× 310).

Note in B the absence of hyperchromatic cells, the hypochromatic condition of all the Purkinje cells, and the almost complete disintegration of the cells indicated by arrows.

of the brain be discharged by injury under anesthesia or by ordinary muscular exertion, identical morphologic changes are seen in the nerve-cells.   In shock from injury (Fig. 2), in exhaustion from overwork (Hodge and Dolley) (Fig. 4),

Fig. 5.

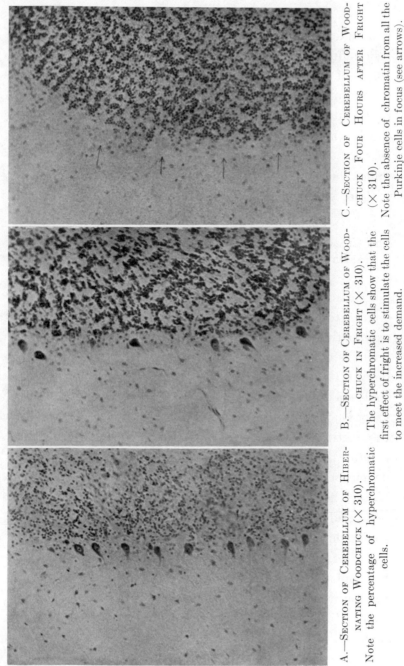

A.—Section of Cerebellum of Hibernating Woodchuck (× 310). Note the percentage of hyperchromatic cells.

B.—Section of Cerebellum of Woodchuck in Fright (× 310). The hyperchromatic cells show that the first effect of fright is to stimulate the cells to meet the increased demand.

C.—Section of Cerebellum of Woodchuck Four Hours after Fright (× 310). Note the absence of chromatin from all the Purkinje cells in focus (see arrows).

11

and in exhaustion from pure fear (Fig. 5), the resultant general functional weakness is similar—in each case a certain length of time is required to effect recovery, and in each there are morphologic changes in the brain-cells. It is quite clear that in each of these cases the altered function and form of the brain-cells are due to an *excessive discharge of nervous energy*. This brings us to the next question: What determines the discharge of energy as a result of trauma with or without inhalation anesthesia?

The Cause of the Discharge of Nervous Energy as a Result of Trauma under Inhalation Anesthesia and under Normal Conditions

I looked into this problem from many viewpoints and there seemed to be no solution until it occurred to me to seek the explanation in certain of the postulates which make up the doctrine of evolution. I realize fully the difficulty and the danger in attempting to reach the generalization which I shall make later and in the hypothesis I shall propose, for there is, of course, no direct final proof of the truth of even the doctrine of evolution. It is idle to consider any experimental research into the cause of phenomena that have developed by natural selection during millions of years. Nature herself has made the experiments on a world-wide scale and the data are before us for interpretation. Darwin could do no more than to collect all available facts and then to frame the hypothesis by which the facts were best harmonized. Sherrington, that masterly physiologist, in his volume entitled "The Integrative Action of the Nervous System," shows clearly how the central nervous system was built up in the process of evolution. Sherrington has made free use of Darwin's doctrine in explaining physiologic functions, just as anatomists have extensively utilized it in the explanation of the genesis of anatomic forms. I shall assume, therefore, that the discharge of nervous energy is accomplished by the application of the laws of inheritance and association, and I conclude that this hypothesis will explain many clinical phenomena. I shall now present such evidence in favor of this hypothesis as time and my limitations will admit, after which I shall point out certain clinical facts that may be explained by this hypothesis.

According to the doctrine of evolution, every function owes its origin to natural selection in the struggle for existence. In the lower and simpler forms of animal life, indeed, in our human progenitors as well, existence depended principally upon the success with which three great purposes were achieved: (1) Self-defense against or escape from enemies; (2) the acquisition of food; and (3) procreation; and these were virtually the only purposes for which nervous energy was discharged. In its last analysis, in a biologic sense, this statement holds true of man today. Disregarding for the present the expenditure of energy for procuring food and for procreation, let us consider the discharge of energy for self-preservation. The mechanisms for self-defense which we now possess were developed in the course of vast periods of time through innumerable intermediary stages from those possessed by the lowest forms of life. One would suppose, therefore, that we must now be in possession of mechanisms which still discharge energy on adequate stimulation, but which are not suited to our present needs. We shall point out some examples of such unnecessary mechanisms. As Sherrington has stated, our skin, in which are implanted

many receptors for receiving specific stimuli which are transmitted to the brain, is interposed between ourselves and
the environment in which we are immersed. When these
stimuli reach the brain, there is a specific response, principally in the form of muscular action. Now, each receptor
can be adequately stimulated only by the particular factor
or factors in the environment which created the necessity
for the existence of that receptor. Thus there have arisen
receptors for touch, for temperature, for pain, etc. The
receptors for pain have been designated *nociceptors* (nocuous
or harmful) by Sherrington.

On the basis of natural selection, nociceptors could have
developed in only those regions of the body which have been
exposed to injury during long periods of time. On this
ground the finger, because it is exposed, should have many
nociceptors, while the brain, though the most important
organ of the body, should have no nociceptors because,
during a vast period of time, it has been protected by a skull.
Realizing that this point is a crucial one, Dr. Sloan and I
made a series of careful experiments. The cerebral hemispheres of dogs were exposed by removing the skull and dura
under ether and local anesthesia. Then various portions
of the hemispheres were slowly but completely destroyed
by rubbing them with pieces of gauze. In some instances
a hemisphere was destroyed by burning. In no case was
there more than a slight response of the centers governing
circulation and respiration, and no morphologic change was
noted in an histologic study of the brain-cells of the uninjured hemisphere. The experiment was as completely
negative as were the experiments on the "spinal dog."
Clinically I have confirmed these experimental findings

when I have explored the brains of conscious patients with a probe to determine the presence of brain tumors. Such explorations elicited neither pain nor any evidence of altered physiologic functions. The brain, therefore, contains no mechanism—no nociceptors—the direct stimulation of which can cause a discharge of nervous energy in a self-defensive action. That is to say, direct injury of the brain can cause no purposeful nerve-muscular action, while direct injury of the finger does cause purposeful nerve-muscular action. In like manner, the deeper portions of the spinal region have been sheltered from trauma and they, too, show but little power of causing a discharge of nervous energy on receiving trauma. The various tissues and organs of the body are differently endowed with injury receptors—the nociceptors of Sherrington. The abdomen and chest when traumatized stand first in their facility for causing the discharge of nervous energy, *i. e., they stand first in shock production.* Then follow the extremities, the neck, and the back. It is an interesting fact also that different types of trauma elicit different responses as far as the consequent discharge of energy is concerned.

Because it is such a commonplace observation, one scarcely realizes the importance of the fact that clean-cut wounds inflicted by a razor-like knife cause the least reaction, while a tearing, crushing trauma causes the greatest response. It is a suggestive fact that the greatest shock is produced by any technic which imitates the methods of attack and of slaughter used by the carnivora. *In the course of evolution, injuries thus produced may well have been the predominating type of traumata to which our progenitors were subjected.*

In one particular respect there is an analogy between the

response to trauma of some parts of the body of the individuals of a species susceptible to shock and the response to trauma of the individuals in certain other great divisions of the animal kingdom. Natural selection has protected the crustaceans against their enemies by protective armor, *e. g.*, the turtle and the armadillo; to the birds, it has given sharp eyes and wings, as, for instance, the wild goose; to another species—the skunk—it has given a noisome odor for its protection. The turtle, protected by its armor against trauma, is in a very similar position to that of the sheltered brain of man; and, like the brain, the turtle does not respond to trauma by an especially active self-protective nerve-muscular response, but merely withdraws its head and legs within the armored protection. It is proverbially difficult to exhaust or to kill this animal by trauma. The brain and other phylogenetically sheltered parts likewise give no exhausting self-protective nerve-muscular response to trauma. The skunk is quite effectively protected from violence by its peculiar odor. This is indicated not only by the protective value of the odor itself, but also by the fact that the skunk has no efficient nerve-muscular mechanism for escape or defense; it can neither run fast nor can it climb a tree. Moreover, in encounters it shows no fear and backs rather than runs. The armadillo rolls itself into a ball for defense. On these premises we should conclude that the turtle, the armadillo, and the skunk have fewer nociceptors than has a dog or man, and that they would show less response to trauma. In two carefully conducted experiments on skunks and two on armadillos (an insufficient number) the energy discharged in response to severe and protracted trauma of the abdominal viscera was very much less than in similar experiments on dogs, opossums, pigs, sheep, and rabbits. It was indeed relatively difficult to exhaust the skunks and armadillos by trauma. These experiments are too few to be conclusive, but they are of some value and furnish an

FIG. 6.—TIGER AND COBRA.

The attitude of each animal is that of watchful approach rather than of fear, an emotion unfelt by the cobra guarded by his venom, or by the tiger conscious of his strong and powerful equipment for defense.

excellent lead. It seems more than a coincidence that proneness to fear, distribution of nociceptors, and susceptibility to shock go hand-in-hand in these comparative observations (Figs. 6, 7, and 8).

2

The discharge of energy caused by an adequate mechanical stimulation of the nociceptors is best explained in accordance with the law of phylogenetic association.   That is, injuries

FIG. 7.—CONTEST BETWEEN A DEER AND A DOG.

Compare the intense stimulation and fearful excitement manifested by these animals with the calm control of the animals in Fig. 6.

awaken those reflex actions which by natural selection have been developed for the purpose of self-protection. Adequate stimulation of the nociceptors for pain is not the only means by which a discharge of nervous energy is caused.

A   *B*

FIG. 8.—THE FINISH OF A RACE.

The contrast between animals in Figs. 6 and 7 finds its analogy in a comparison of these runners—*A*, poorly equipped by training and fearful of the result, shows every evidence of exhaustion; while *B*, confident in the strength given by superior training, wins the race with ease.

Nervous energy may be discharged also by adequate stimulation of the various ticklish regions of the body; the entire skin surface of the body contains delicate ticklish receptors. These receptors are closely related to the nociceptors for pain, and their adequate stimulation by an insect-like touch causes a discharge of energy,—a nerve-muscular reaction,— resembling that developed for the purpose of brushing off insects. This reflex is similar to the scratch reflex in the dog. The discharge of energy is almost wholly independent of the will and is a self-protective action in the same sense as is the response to pain stimuli. The ear in man and in animals is acutely ticklish, the adequate stimulus being any foreign body, especially a buzzing, insect-like contact. The discharge of nervous energy in horses and in cattle on adequate stimulation of the ticklish receptors of the ear is so extraordinary that in the course of evolution it must have been of great importance to the safety of the animal. A similar ticklish zone guards the nasal chambers, the discharge of energy here taking a form which effectively dislodges the foreign body. The larynx is exquisitely ticklish, and, in response to any adequate stimulus, energy is discharged in the production of a vigorous cough. The mouth and pharynx have active receptors which cause the rejection of noxious substances. The conjunctival reflex, though not classed as ticklish, is a most efficient self-protective reflex. I assume that there is no doubt as to the relation between the adequate stimuli and the nerve-muscular response of the various ticklish receptors of the surface of the skin, of the ear, the nose, the eye, and the larynx. These mechanisms were developed by natural selection as protective measures against the intrusion of insects and foreign bodies into regions of great importance. The discharge of energy in these instances is in accordance with the laws of inheritance and association. The other ticklish points which are capable of discharging vast amounts of energy are the lateral chest-wall, the abdomen, the loins, the neck, and the soles of the feet. The type of adequate stimuli of the soles of the feet, the dis-

FIG. 9.—CONTEST BETWEEN ANT-BEAR AND PUMA.

This shows the attack with teeth and claws upon unprotected parts, and illustrates the method by which deep, ticklish points were developed and why trauma of these parts produces the greatest shock.

tribution of the ticklish points upon them, and the associated response, leave no doubt that these ticklish points were long ago established as a means of protection from injury. Under present conditions they are of little value to man.

The adequate stimulus for the ticklish points of the ribs, the loins, the abdomen, and the neck is deep isolated pressure, probably the most adequate being pressure by a tooth-shaped body. The response to tickling in these regions is actively and obviously self-defensive. The horse discharges

FIG. 10.—BEAR CUBS AT PLAY.
They are clawing and biting each other in ticklish points and thus recapitulating ancestral battles. (Photo by Underwood and Underwood, N. Y.)

energy in the form of a kick; the dog wriggles and makes a counter-bite; the man makes efforts at defense and escape.

There is strong evidence that the deep ticklish points of the body were developed through vast periods of fighting with teeth and claws (Fig. 9). Even puppies at play bite each other in their ticklish points and thus give a recapitulation of their ancestral battles and of the real battles to come (Fig.

10). The mere fact that animals fight effectively in the dark and always according to the habit of their species supports the belief that the fighting of animals is not an intellectual but a reflex process. There are no rules which govern the conduct of a fight between animals. The events follow each other with such kaleidoscopic rapidity that the process is but a series of automatic stimulations and physiologic reactions. Whatever their significance, therefore, it is certain that man did not come either accidentally or without purpose into possession of the deep ticklish regions of his chest and abdomen. Should any one doubt the vast power that adequate stimulation of these regions possesses in causing the discharge of energy, let him be bound hand and foot and vigorously tickled for an hour. What would happen? He would be as completely exhausted as though he had experienced a major surgical operation or had run a Marathon race.

A close analogy to the reflex process in the fighting of animals is shown in the rôle played by the sexual receptors in conjugation. Adequate stimulation of either of these two distinct groups of receptors, the sexual and the noci, causes specific behavior—the one toward embrace, the other toward repulsion. Again, one of the most peremptory causes of the discharge of energy is that due to an attempt to obstruct forcibly the mouth and the nose so that asphyxia is threatened. Under such conditions neither friend nor foe is trusted, and a desperate struggle for air ensues. It will be readily granted that the reactions to prevent suffocation were established for the purpose of self-preservation, but the discharge of nerve-muscular energy to this particular end is no more specific and no more shows adaptive qualities than do the preceding examples. Even the proposal to bind one down hand and foot excites resentment, a feeling originally suggested by the need for self-preservation. No patient views with equanimity the application of shackles as a preparation for anesthesia.

We have now considered some of the causes of those discharges of nervous energy which result from various types of harmful physical contact, and have referred to the analogous, though antithetical, response to the stimulation of the sexual receptors. The response to the adequate stimuli of each of the several receptors is a discharge of nerve-muscular energy of a specific type; that is, there is one type of response for the ear, one for the larynx, one for the pharynx, another for the nose, another for the eye, another for the deep ticklish points of the chest and the abdomen, quite another for the delicate tickling of the skin, and still another type of response to sexual stimuli.

According to Sherrington, a given receptor has a low threshold for only one, its own specific stimulus, and a high threshold for all others; that is, the doors that guard the nerve-paths to the brain are opened only when the proper password is received. According to Sherrington's law, the individual as a whole responds to but one stimulus at a time, that is, only one stimulus occupies the nerve-paths which carry the impulses as a result of which acts are performed, i. e., the final common path. As soon as a stronger stimulus reaches the brain it dispossesses whatever other stimulus is then occupying the final common path—the path of action. The various receptors have a definite order of precedence over each other (Sherrington). For example, the impulse from the delicate ticklish points of the skin, whose adequate stimulus is an insect-like contact, could not successfully compete for the final common path with the stimulus of a nociceptor. The stimulus of a fly on the nose would be at once superseded by the crushing of a finger. In quick succession do the various receptors (Sherrington) occupy the final common path, but each stimulus is for the time the sole possessor, hence the nervous system is integrated (connected) to act as a whole. Each individual at every moment of life has a limited amount of dischargeable nervous energy. This energy is at the disposal of any stimulus that obtains possession of the final common path, and results in the performance of an act. Each discharge of energy is subtracted from the sum total of stored energy and, whether the subtractions are made by the excitation of nociceptors by trauma, by tickling, by fighting, by fear, by flight, or by the excitation of sexual receptors, by any of these singly or in combination with others, the sum total of the expenditure of energy, if large enough, produces exhaustion. Apparently there is no distinction between that state of exhaustion which is due to the discharge of nervous energy in response to trauma and that due to other causes. The manner of the discharge of energy is specific for each type of stimulation. On this conception, traumatic shock takes its place as a natural phenomenon and is divested of its mask of mystery.

The Discharge of Energy through Stimulation of the Distance Receptors, or through Representation of Injury (Psychic)

We will now turn from the discussion of the discharge of nervous energy by mechanical stimuli to the discharge of energy through mental perception. *Phylogenetic* association may result from stimulation of the distance receptors through sight, hearing, smell, or by a representation of physical experiences, as well as from physical contact. The effect upon the organism of the representation of injury or of the perception of danger through the distance receptors is designated *fear*. Fear is as widely distributed in nature as is its cause, that is, fear is as widely distributed as injury. Animals under the stimulus of fear, according to W. T. Hornaday, not only may exhibit preternatural strength, but also may show strategy of the highest order, a strategy not seen under the influence of a lesser stimulus. In some animals fear is so intense that it defeats escape; this is especially true in the case of birds in the presence of snakes. The power of flight has endowed the bird with an easy means of escape from snakes, especially when the encounter is in the tops of trees. Here the snake must move cautiously, else he will lose his equilibrium; his method of attack is by stealth. When the snake has stalked its prey, the bird is often so overcome by fear that it cannot fly and so becomes an easy victim (Fig. 11). The phenomena of fear are described by Darwin as follows:

"Fear is often preceded by astonishment, and is so near akin to it that both lead to the senses of sight and hearing being instantly aroused. In both cases the eyes and mouth are widely opened and the eyebrows raised. The frightened man at first stands like a statue, motionless and breathless, or crouches down as if instinctively to escape observation. The heart beats quickly and violently, so that it palpitates or knocks against the ribs. * * * That the skin is much affected under the sense of great fear we see in the marvelous and inexplicable manner in which perspiration immediately exudes from it. This exudation is all the more remarkable as the surface is then cold, and hence the term, 'a cold sweat'; whereas the sudorific glands are properly

Fig. 11.—Bird Charmed by Snake.
Fear so dominates the bird that it is unable to fly.

excited into action when the surface is heated. The hairs also on the skin stand erect, and the superficial muscles shiver. In connection with the disturbed action of the heart, the breathing is hurried. The salivary glands act imperfectly; the mouth becomes dry, and is often opened and shut. I have also noticed that under slight fear there is a strong tendency to yawn. One of the best-marked symptoms is the trembling of all the muscles of the body; and this is often first seen in the lips. From this cause, and from the dryness of the mouth, the voice becomes husky and indistinct, or may altogether fail. * * * As fear increases into agony of terror, we behold, as under all violent emotions, diversified results. The heart beats wildly, or may fail to act and faintness ensues; there is death-like pallor; the breathing is labored; the wings of the nostrils are widely dilated; 'there is a gasping and convulsive motion of the lips, a tremor on the hollow cheek, a gulping and catching of the throat'; the uncovered and protruding eyeballs are fixed on the object of terror; or they may roll restlessly from side to side. * * * The pupils are said to be enormously dilated. All the muscles of the body may become rigid, or may be thrown into convulsive movements. The hands are alternately clenched and opened, often with a twitching movement. The arms may be protruded, as if to avert some dreadful danger, or may be thrown wildly over the head. * * * In other cases there is a sudden and uncontrollable tendency to headlong flight; and so strong is this that the boldest soldiers may be seized with a sudden panic. As fear rises to an extreme pitch, the dreadful scream of terror is heard. Great beads of sweat stand on the skin. All the muscles of the body are relaxed. Utter prostration soon follows, and the mental powers fail. The intestines are affected. The sphincter muscles cease to act and no longer retain the contents of the body. * * *

Men, during numberless generations, have endeavored to escape from their enemies or danger by headlong flight, or by violently struggling with them; and such great exertions will have caused the heart to beat rapidly, the breathing

FIG. 12.—PHOTO SHOWING FACIES OF PERSON OBSESSED BY FEAR.

to be hurried, the chest to heave, and the nostrils to be dilated. As these exertions have often been prolonged to the last extremity, the final result will have been utter prostration, pallor, perspiration, trembling of all the muscles, or their complete relaxation. And now, whenever the emotion of fear is strongly felt, though it may not lead to any exertion, the same results tend to reappear, through the force of inheritance and association"* (Fig. 12).

In an experimental research, we found evidence that the physiologic phenomena of fear have a physical basis. This evidence is found in the morphologic alterations in the brain-cells, which are similar to those observed in certain stages of surgical shock and in fatigue from muscular exertion (Figs. 2, 4, 5, and 13). For the present, we shall assume that fear is a *representation* of trauma. Because fear was created by trauma, fear causes a discharge of the energy of the nervous system by the law of phylogenetic association. The almost universal fear of snakes, of blood, and of death and dead bodies may have such a phylogenetic origin. It was previously stated that under the stimulus of fear animals show preternatural strength. An analysis of the phenomena of fear shows that, as far as can be determined, all the functions of the body requiring the expenditure of energy, and which are of no direct assistance in the effort toward self-preservation, are suspended. In the voluntary expenditure of muscular energy, as in the chase, the suspension of other functions is by no means so complete. Fear and trauma may drain to the last dreg the dischargeable nervous energy, and, therefore, the greatest possible exhaustion may be produced by fear and trauma.

Summation

In the discharge of energy, summation plays an important rôle. Summation is attained by the repetition of stimuli at such a rate that each succeeding stimulus is applied before

* Darwin: Expression of the Emotions in Man and Animals.

FIG. 13.

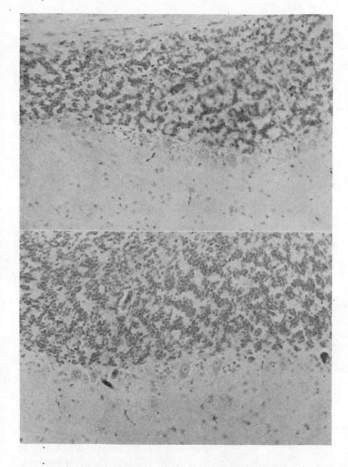

A.—Section of Cerebellum of Rabbit—Normal (× 310).

B.—Section of Cerebellum of Rabbit Showing the Lasting Effects of Fright (× 310).

The animal had recovered, but the cells are still hypochromatic and some have been exhausted beyond the power of recuperation.

C.—Section of Cerebellum of Rabbit Showing Effects of Repeated Fright (× 310).

Note the fatigued cells and the faint traces of exhausted cells.

31

the nerve-cells have returned to the resting stage from the preceding stimulus. If drops of water fall upon the skin from a sufficient height to cause the slightest unpleasant sensation, and at such a rate that before the effect of the stimulus of one drop has passed another drop falls in precisely the same spot, there will be felt a gradually increasing painful sensation which finally becomes unbearable. This is summation of stimuli. When, for a long time, a patient requires frequent painful wound dressings, there is a gradual increase in the acuteness of the pain of the receptors. This is caused by summation. In a larger sense, the entire behavior of the individual gives considerable evidence of summation, e. g., in the training of athletes, the rhythmic discharge of muscular energy at such intervals that the resting stage is not reached before a new exercise is given results in a gradual ascent in efficiency until the maximum is reached. This is summation, and summation plays a large rôle in the development of both normal and pathologic phenomena.

We have now pointed out the manner in which at least a part of the nervous energy of man may be discharged. The integrative action of the nervous system and the discharge of nervous energy by phylogenetic association may be illustrated by their analogy to the action of an electric automobile. The electric automobile is composed of four principal parts: The motor and the wheels (the muscular system and the skeleton); the cells of the battery containing stored electricity (brain-cells, nervous energy); the controller, which is connected with the cells by wiring (the receptors and the nerve-fibers); and an accelerator for increasing the electric discharge (thyroid gland?). The machine is so constructed that it acts as a whole for the accomplishment of a single purpose. When the controller is adjusted for going ahead (adequate stimulus of a receptor), then the conducting paths (the final common path) for the accomplishment of that purpose are all open to the flow of the current from the battery, and the vehicle is integrated to go ahead. It spends its energy to that end and is closed to all other impulses. When the controller is set for reverse, by this adequate stimulus the machine is integrated to back, and the battery is closed to all other impulses. Whether integrated for going forward or backward, if the battery be discharged at a proper rate until exhausted, the cells, though possessing no more power (fatigue), have sustained no further impairment of their elements than that of normal wear and tear. Furthermore, they may be restored to normal activity by recharging (rest). If the vehicle be placed against a stone wall, and the controller be placed at high-speed (trauma and fear), and if the accelerator be used as well (thyroid secretion?), though the machine will not move, not only will the battery soon be exhausted, but the battery elements themselves will be seriously damaged (exhaustion —surgical shock).

We have now presented some evidence that nervous energy is discharged by the adequate stimulation of one or more of the various receptors that have been developed in the course of evolution. In response to an adequate stimulus, the nervous system is integrated for a specific purpose by the stimulated receptor, and but one stimulus at a time has possession of the final common path—the nerve mechanisms for action. The most numerous receptors are those for harmful contact; these are the nociceptors. The effect

3

of the adequate stimulus of a nociceptor is like that of pressing an electric button that sets great machinery in motion.

With this conception, the human body may be likened to a musical instrument—an organ—the keyboard of which is composed of the various receptors, upon which environment plays the many tunes of life; and written within ourselves in symbolic language is the history of our evolution. The skin may be the "Rosetta Stone" which furnishes the key.

Anoci-association

By the law of phylogenetic association, we are now prepared to make a practical application of the principles of the discharge of nervous energy. In the case of a surgical operation, if fear be excluded and if the nerve-paths between the field of operation and the brain be blocked with cocain,* no discharge of energy will be caused by the operation; hence no shock, no exhaustion, can result. Under such conditions the nervous system is protected against noci-association, resulting from noci-perception or from an adequate stimulation of nociceptors. The state of the patient in whom all noci-associations are excluded can be described only by coining a new word. That word is "anoci-association" (Fig. 14).

The difference between anesthesia and anoci-association is that, although *inhalation anesthesia* confers the beneficent loss of consciousness and freedom from pain, it does not prevent the nerve impulses from reaching and influencing the brain, and therefore does not prevent surgical shock nor the train of later nervous impairments so well described by Mumford. *Anoci-association* excludes fear, pain, shock, and post-

* See footnote, page 4.

operative neuroses. *Anoci-association* is accomplished by combining the special management of patients (applied

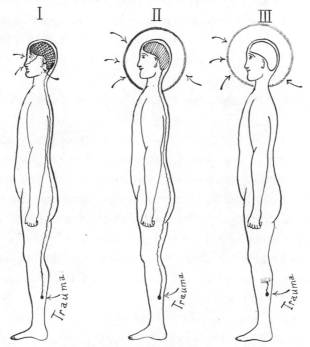

FIG. 14.—SCHEMATIC DRAWING ILLUSTRATING PROTECTIVE EFFECT OF ANOCI-ASSOCIATION.

    I. Conscious patient in whom auditory, visual, olfactory, and traumatic noci-impulses reach the brain.

    II. Patient under inhalation anesthesia in whom only traumatic noci-impulses reach the brain.

    III. Patient under complete *anoci-association;* auditory, visual, and olfactory impulses are excluded from the brain by the inhalation anesthesia; traumatic impulses from the seat of injury are blocked by novocain.

psychology), morphin, inhalation anesthesia, and local anesthesia.

We have now presented in summary much of the mass of experimental and clinical evidence we have accumulated in support of our principal theme, which is that the discharge of nervous energy is accomplished in accordance with the law of phylogenetic association. If this point seems to have been emphasized unduly, it is because we expect to rear upon this foundation a clinical structure. How does this hypothesis apply to surgical operations?

Prevention of Shock by the Application of the Principle of Anoci-association

Upon this hypothesis a new principle in operative surgery is founded, *i. e.*, operation during the state of *anoci-association*. Assuming that no unfavorable effect is produced by the anesthetic and that there is no hemorrhage, the cells of the brain cannot be exhausted in the course of a surgical operation except by fear or by trauma, or by both. Fear may be excluded by narcotics and special management until the patient is rendered unconscious by inhalation anesthesia. Then if, in addition to inhalation anesthesia, the nerve-paths between the brain and the field of operation are blocked with cocain,* the patient will be placed in the beneficent state of *anoci-association*, and at the completion of the operation will be as free from shock as at the beginning. In so-called "fair risks" such precautions may not be necessary, but in cases handicapped by infections, by anemia, by previous shock, and by Graves' disease, etc., anoci-association may become vitally important.

Graves' Disease

By applying the principle of the discharge of nervous energy by phylogenetic association, and by making the

* See footnote, page 4.

additional hypothesis that in the discharge of nervous energy the thyroid gland is stimulated through the nervous system, we can explain many of the phenomena of Graves' disease and may possibly discover some of the factors which explain both its genesis and its cure.

In the wild state of animal life in which only the fittest survive in the struggle for existence, every point of advantage has its value. An animal engaged in battle or in a desperate effort to escape will be able to give a better account of itself if it have some means of accelerating the discharge of energy —some influence like that of pouring oil upon the kindling fire. There is evidence, though perhaps it is not conclusive, that such an influence is exerted by the thyroid gland. In myxedema, a condition characterized by a lack of thyroid secretion, there is dulness of the reflexes and of the intellect, a lowered muscular power, and generally a sluggish discharge of energy. In Graves' disease there is an excessive production of thyroid secretion. In this disease the reflexes are increased, the discharge of energy is greatly facilitated, and metabolism is at a maximum. The same phenomena occur also after the administration of thyroid extract in large doses to normal subjects. In the course of sexual activities there is an increased action of the thyroid, which is indicated by an increase in its size and vascularity. That in fear and in injury the thyroid, in cases of Graves' disease, is probably stimulated to increased activity is indicated by the increased activity of the thyroid circulation, by an increase in the size of the gland, by the histologic appearance of activity in the nuclei of the cells, and by an increase of the toxic symptoms. Finally, Asher has stated that electric stimulation of the nerve supply of the thyroid causes an increased secretion.

The origin of many cases of Graves' disease is closely associated with some of the causes of the discharge of nervous energy, depressive influences especially, such as nervous shocks, worry and nervous strain, disappointment in love, business reverses, illness and death of relatives and friends. The association of thyroid activity with procreation is well known, hence the coincidence of a strain of overwork or of fear with the sexual development of maturing girls is obviously favorable to the incidence of Graves' disease. The presence of a colloid goiter is a suitable soil for the development of Graves' disease, and I fully recognize also the evidence that infection or auto-intoxication may be contributing factors and must be assigned their rôle.

I have never known a case of Graves' disease to be caused by success or happiness alone, or by hard physical labor unattended by psychic strain, or to be the result of energy voluntarily discharged. Some cases seem to have had their origin in overdosage with thyroid extract in too vigorous an attempt to cure a colloid goiter. One of the most striking characteristics of Graves' disease is the patient's loss of control and his increased susceptibility to stimuli, especially to trauma and to fear and to the administration of thyroid extract. It has been shown that the various causes of the discharge of nervous energy produce alterations in the nervous system and probably in the thyroid gland. This is especially true of the fear stimulus, and has been clearly demonstrated in the brains of rabbits which had been subjected to fear alone (Fig. 13). Of special interest was the effect of daily fright. In this case the brain-cells showed a distinct change, although the animal had been subjected to no fear for twenty-four hours before it was killed (Fig. 13 C).

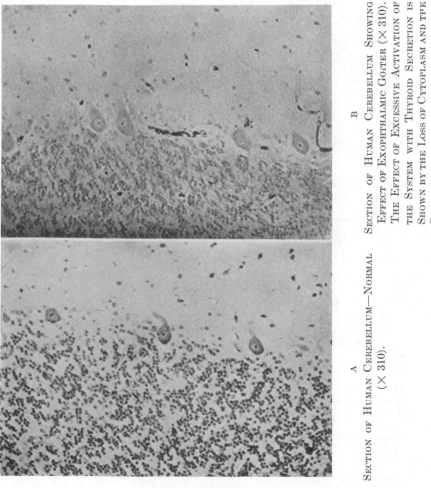

A

SECTION OF HUMAN CEREBELLUM—NORMAL (× 310).

B

SECTION OF HUMAN CEREBELLUM SHOWING EFFECT OF EXOPHTHALMIC GOITER (× 310). THE EFFECT OF EXCESSIVE ACTIVATION OF THE SYSTEM WITH THYROID SECRETION IS SHOWN BY THE LOSS OF CYTOPLASM AND THE DEGENERATION OF THE PURKINJE CELLS.

Now, a great distinction between man and the lower animals is the greater control man has acquired over his actions. This quality of control, having been phylogenetically most recently acquired, is the most vulnerable to various *nocuous* influences. The result of a constant noci-integration may be a wearing-out of the control cells of the brain. In a typical

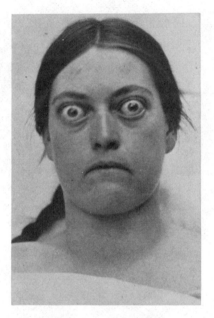

FIG. 16.—TYPICAL CASE OF EXOPHTHALMIC GOITER SHOWING CHARACTERISTIC FACIES.

case of Graves' disease a marked morphologic change in the brain-cells has been demonstrated (Fig. 15). As has been previously stated, the origin of many cases of Graves' disease is associated with some noci-influence. If this influence causes stimulation of both the brain and the thyroid, its excessive action may cause impairment of the brain and also hyperplasia of the thyroid. As self-control is impaired, fear obtains an ascendency and, *pari passu*, stimulates the thyroid still more actively (Fig. 16). Finally, the fear of the disease itself becomes a noci-stimulus. As the thyroid secretion causes an increase in the facility with which nervous energy is discharged, a pathologic reciprocal interaction is established between the brain and the thyroid. The effect of the constantly recurring stimulus of the noci-influence is heightened by summation. This reciprocal goading may continue until either the brain or the thyroid is destroyed. If the original noci-stimulus is withdrawn before the fear of the disease becomes too strong, and before too much injury to the brain and the thyroid has been inflicted, a spontaneous cure may result. Recovery may be greatly facilitated by complete therapeutic rest. A cure implies the return of the brain-cells to their normal state, with the reëstablishment of the normal self-control and the restoration of the thyroid to its normal state, when the impulses of daily life will once more have possession of the final common path and the noci-influence will be dispossessed. The discovery of the real cause of a given case of Graves' disease is frequently difficult because it may be of a painful personal nature. Of extreme interest is the fact that, in the acute stage, the patient may be unable to refer to the exciting cause without exhibiting an exacerbation of the symptoms of the disease. I presume no case should be regarded as cured until reference can be made to its cause without an abnormal reaction. It has been established that in Graves' disease injury to any part of the body, even under inhalation anesthesia, causes an exacerbation of the disease. Fear alone may cause an acute exacerbation. These acute exacerbations are frequently designated "hyperthyroidism" and are the special hazard of operation.

In applying the principle of anoci-association in operations on patients with Graves' disease there is scarcely a change in the pulse, in the respiration, or in the nervous state at the close of the operation. I know no remedy which can obviate the effect of the inflowing stimuli from the wound after the cocain* has worn off.† It is necessary, therefore,

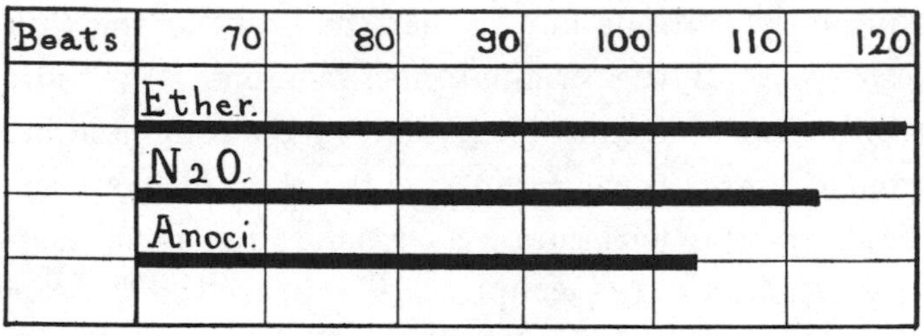

Beats	70	80	90	100	110	120
Ether.						
N₂O.						
Anoci.						

The Pulse.

Each heavy line represents the average 5 P. M. pulse-rate of ten patients during the first four days after operation.

FIG. 17.—COMPARATIVE CLINICAL RESULTS OF CONSECUTIVE THYROIDECTOMIES PERFORMED UNDER ETHER, UNDER NITROUS-OXID-OXYGEN ALONE, AND UNDER COMPLETE *Anoci-association*.

not to venture too far in serious cases. Since the adoption of this new method (anoci-association) my operative results have been so vastly improved that I now rarely regard any case of Graves' disease as inoperable, at least to the extent of contraindicating a double ligation (Fig. 17).

If we believe that, in accordance with the law of phylo-genetic association, a continuous stimulation of both the brain and the thyroid gland, accelerated by summation,

* See footnote, page 4.

† In later papers and in "Anoci-association" (Crile and Lower) methods of combating postoperative hyperthyroidism are fully discussed.

plays a rôle in the establishment of the pathologic interaction seen in Graves' disease, then it is but the next step to assume that if the nerve connection between the brain and the thyroid be severed, or if the lobe be excised and the patient reinforced by a sojourn in a sanatorium or in some environment free from former noci-associations, he may be restored to normal health, provided that the brain-cells, the heart, or other essential organs have not suffered irreparable damage. There are still many missing links in the solution of this problem, and the foregoing hypotheses are not offered as final, although from the viewpoint of the surgeon many of the phenomena of this disease are explicable.

Sexual Neurasthenia

The state of sexual neurasthenia is in many respects analogous to that of Graves' disease. In the sexual reflexes, summation leads to a hyperexcitability by psychic and mechanical stimuli of a specific type which is analogous to the hyperexcitability in Graves' disease under trauma and fear; the explanation of both conditions is based on the laws of the discharge of energy by phylogenetic association and summation. It would be interesting to observe the effect of interrupting the nerve impulses from the field of the sexual receptors by injections of alcohol, or by other agencies, so as to exclude the associational stimuli until the nervous mechanism has again become restored to its normal condition.

Interpretation of Some of the Phenomena of Certain Diseases of the Abdomen in Accordance with the Hypothesis of Phylogenetic Association

The law of phylogenetic association seems to explain many of the phenomena of certain lesions in the abdominal cavity. The nociceptors in the abdomen, like nociceptors elsewhere, have been established as a result of some kind of injury to which during vast periods of time this region has been frequently exposed. On this premise, we should at once conclude that there are no nociceptors for heat within the abdomen because, during countless years, the intra-abdominal region never came into contact with heat. That this inference is correct is shown by the fact that the application of a thermocautery to the intestines when completing a colostomy in a conscious patient is absolutely painless. One would conclude also that there are no touch receptors in the abdominal viscera, and therefore no sense of touch in the peritoneum. Just as the larynx, the ear, the nose, the sole of the foot, and the skin have all developed the specific type of nociceptors which are adapted for their specific protective purposes, and which, when adequately stimulated, respond in a specific manner in accordance with the law of phylogenetic association, so the abdominal viscera have developed equally specific nociceptors as a protection against specific nocuous influences. The principal harmful influences to which the abdominal viscera have been exposed during vast periods of time are deep tearing injuries by teeth and claws in the innumerable struggles of our progenitors with each other and with their enemies (Fig. 9); peritonitis caused by perforations of the intestinal tract from ulcers, injuries, appendicitis, gall-stones, etc.; and overdistention of the hollow viscera by various forms of obstruction. Whatever may be the explanation, it is a fact that the type of trauma which results from fighting corresponds closely with that which causes the most shock in the experimental laboratory. Division of the intestines with a sharp knife causes no pain, but pulling on the mesentery elicits pain. Ligating the stump of the appendix causes sharp, cramp-like pains. Sharp division of the gall-bladder causes no pain, but distention, which is the gall-bladder's most common pathologic state, produces pain. Distention of the intestine causes great pain, but sharp cutting or burning causes none. In the abdominal viscera, as in the superficial parts, nociceptors have presumably been developed by specific harmful influences and each nociceptor is open to stimulation only by a stimulus of the particular type that produced it.

As a result of the excitation of nociceptors, with which pain is associated, the routine functions, such as peristalsis, secretion, and absorption are dispossessed from the control of their respective nervous mechanisms, just as they are inhibited by fear. This hypothesis explains the loss of weight, the lassitude, the indigestion, the constipation, and the many alterations in the functions of the various glands and organs of the digestive system in chronic appendicitis. It readily explains also the extraordinary improvement in the digestive functions and the general health which follows the removal of an appendix which is so slightly altered physically that only the clinical results could persuade one that this slight change could be an adequate cause for such far-reaching and important symptoms. This hypothesis explains certain gall-bladder phenomena likewise,—indigestion, loss of weight, disturbed functions, etc.,—and it may supply the explanation of the disturbance caused by an active anal fissure, which is a potent noci-associator, and the consequent disproportionate relief after the trivial operation for its cure. Noci-association would well explain also the great functional disturbances of the viscera which immediately follow abdominal operations.

Postoperative and traumatic neuroses are at once explained on the ground of noci-association, the resulting strain from which, upon the brain-cells, causes in them physical lesions. If one were placed against a wall and were looking into the gun muzzles of a squad of soldiers, and were told that there were nine chances out of ten that he would not be killed outright when the volley was fired, would it help him to be told that he must not be afraid? Such an experience would be written indelibly on his brain. This corresponds closely to the position in which some surgical patients are placed. In railway wrecks, we can readily understand the striking difference between the after-effects in the passengers who were conscious at the time of the accident and those who were asleep or drunk. In the latter the noci-perceptors and receptors were not aroused, hence their immunity to the nervous shock. In the functional disturbances of the pelvic organs, association and summation may play a large rôle. On this hypothesis many cases of neurasthenia may well be explained. From the behavior of the individual as a whole we may well conclude that summation is but a scientific expression for "nagging." Many other pathologic phenomena may be explained in a similar manner. Thus we can understand the variations in the gastric analyses in a timid patient alarmed over his condition and afraid of the hospital. He is integrated by fear, and as fear takes precedence over all other impulses, no organ functionates normally. For the same reason, one sees animals in captivity pine away under the dominance of fear. The exposure of a sensitive brain to the naked possibility of death from a surgical operation may be compared to uncovering a photographic plate in the bright sunlight to inspect it before putting it in the camera. This principle explains, too, the physical influence of the physician or surgeon, who, by his *personality*, inspires, like a Kocher, absolute confidence in his patient. The brain, through its power of phylogenetic association, controls many processes that have wholly escaped from the notice of the "practical man." It is in accordance with the law of association that a flower, a word, a touch, a cool breeze, or even the thought of a fishing rod or of a gun, is helpful. On the contrary, all suggestions of despair or misfortune—a corrugated brow, the gloomy silence of despair, or a doubtful word—are equally depressing. In like manner, one could add many illustrations of the symbolism that governs our daily lives. Thus we see that through the laws of inheritance and noci-association, we are able to read a new meaning into the clinical phenomena of various diseases.

Observations on Patients whose Associational Centers are Dulled, and on Diseases and Injuries of Regions not Endowed with Nociceptors

Reversing the order of our reasoning, let us now glance at the patient who is unconscious and who, therefore, has lost much of the power of association. His mouth is usually dry, the digestive processes are at a low ebb, the aroma of food causes no secretion of saliva, tickling the nose causes no sneezing; he catches no cold. The laryngeal reflex is lost and food may be quietly inhaled; the entire process of metabolism is low. The contrast between a man whose associational centers are keen and a man in whom these centers are dulled or lost is the contrast between life and death.

In accordance with the law of adaptation through natural selection, phylogeny, and association, one would expect no pain in abscess of the brain, in abscess of the liver, in pylephlebitis, in infection of the hepatic vessels, in endocarditis. This law explains why there are no nociceptors for cancer, while there are active nociceptors for the acute infections. It is because nature has no helpful response to offer against cancer, while in certain of the acute pyogenic infections the nociceptors force the beneficent physiologic rest.

Could we dispossess ourselves of the shackles of psychology, forget its confusing nomenclature, and view the human brain, as Sherrington has said, "as the organ of, and for the adaptation of nervous reaction," many clinical phenomena would appear in a clearer light.

Natural Selection and Chemical Noci-association in the Infections

Thus far we have considered the behavior of the individual as a whole in his response to a certain type of noci-influences. We have been voicing our argument in terms of physical escape from *gross* physical dangers, or of grappling with *gross nerve-muscular* enemies of the same or of other species. To explain these phenomena we have invoked the aid of the laws of natural selection and phylogenetic association. If our conclusions be correct, then it should follow that in the same laws we may find the explanation of immunity, which, of course, means a defensive response to our *microscopic* enemies. There should be no more difficulty in evolving an efficient army of phagocytes by natural selection, or in developing specific chemical reactions against *microscopic enemies*, than there was in evolving the various nociceptors for our nerve-muscular defense against our *gross enemies*. That immunity is a chemical reaction is no argument against the application of the law of natural selection or of association. What essential difference is there between the chemical defense of the skunk against its *nerve-muscular* enemies and its chemical defense (immunity) against *its microscopic enemies?*

The administration of vaccines becomes the adequate stimulus which awakens phylogenetic association of a chemical nature as a result of which immune bodies are produced.

In discussing this subject I will raise only the question whether or not the specific character of the inaugural symptoms of some infectious diseases may be due to phylogenetic association. These inaugural symptoms are measurably a recapitulation of the leading phenomena of the disease in its completed clinical picture. Thus, the furious initiative symptoms of pneumonia, of peritonitis, or erysipelas, of the exanthemata, are exaggerations of phenomena which are analogous to the phenomena accompanying physical injury and fear of physical violence. Just as the acute phenomena of fear, or those which accompany the adequate stimulation of nociceptors, are recapitulations of phylogenetic struggles,

4

so may the inaugural symptoms of an infection be a similar
phylogenetic recapitulation of the course of the disease. A
certain amount of negative evidence is supplied by a comparison of the response to a dose of toxins with the response
to a dose of a standard drug.   No drug in therapeutic dosage
except the iodin compounds causes a febrile response; no
drug causes a chill; on the other hand, all specific toxins
cause febrile responses and many cause chills.   If a species
of animal had been poisoned by a drug during vast periods
of time, and if natural selection had successfully established
a self-defensive response, then the administration of that
drug would cause a noci-association (chemical), and a specific
reaction analogous to that following the administration of
Coley's toxins might be expected.   Bacterial noci-association probably operates through the same law as that through
which physical noci-association operates.   Natural selection
is impartial, however.   It must be supposed that it acts im-
partially upon the microscopic invader and upon the host.
On this ground one must infer that, in accordance with the
same law of natural selection, the bacteria of acute infections have met by natural selection each advance in the
struggle of the host for immunity.   Hence the fast and
furious struggle between man and his microscopic enemies
merely indicates to what extent natural selection has developed the *attack* and the *defense* respectively.   This
struggle is analogous to the quick and decisive battles of the
carnivora when fighting among themselves or when con-
tending against their ancient enemies.   But when phylogenetically strange animals meet each other, they do not
understand how to conduct a fight: natural selection has not
had the opportunity of teaching them.   The acute infec-

tions have the characteristics of being ancient enemies. On this hypothesis one can understand the high mortality of measles when it is introduced into a new country. By natural selection, measles has become a powerful enemy of the human race, and a race to which this infection is newly introduced has not had the advantage of building up a defense against it by the law of natural selection. May not the phenomena of anaphylaxis be studied on associational lines? Then, too, there may be chemical noci-associations with enemies now extinct, which, like the ticklish points, may still be active on adequate stimulation. This brief reference to the possible relation of the phenomena of the acute infections to the laws of natural selection and of specific chemical noci-association has been made as a suggestion. Since the doctrine of evolution explains all or nothing, I have included many phenomena to see how reasonable or unreasonable such an explanation might be.

Recapitulation

The following are the principal points presented: In operations under inhalation anesthesia the nerve impulses from the trauma reach every part of the brain—the cerebrum that is apparently anesthetized as well as the medulla that is known to remain awake—the proof being the *physiologic* exhaustion of and the *pathologic* change in the nerve-cells. Under ether anesthesia the damage to the nerve-cells is at least four times greater than under nitrous oxid. Inhalation anesthesia is, therefore, but a veneer—a mask that "covers the deep suffering of the patient." The cause of the exhaustion of the brain is the discharge of nervous energy in a futile effort to energize the paralyzed muscles in an attempt to escape from the injury just as if no anesthetic had been given. The exhaustion is, therefore, of the same nature as that from overexertion, but if the nerve-paths connecting the field of operation and the brain be blocked, then there is no discharge of nervous energy from the trauma, and consequently there is no exhaustion, however severe or prolonged the operation may be.

Fear is a factor in many injuries and operations. The phenomena of fear probably are exhibited only by animals whose natural defense is nerve-muscular. The skunk, the porcupine, the turtle, have little or no fear. Fear is born of the innumerable injuries which have been inflicted in the course of evolution. Fear, like trauma, may cause physiologic exhaustion of and morphologic changes in the brain-cells. The representation of injury, which is fear, being elicited by phylogenetic association, may be prevented by the exclusion of the noci-association or by the administration of drugs like morphin and scopolamin, which so impair the associational function of the brain-cells that immunity to fear is established. Animals whose natural defense is in muscular exertion, among which is man, may have their dischargeable nervous energy exhausted by fear alone, or by trauma alone, but most effectively by the combination of both. What is the mechanism of this discharge of energy? It is the adequate stimulation of the nociceptors and the physiologic response for the purpose of self-preservation. According to Sherrington, the nervous system responds in action as a whole and to but one stimulus at a time. The integration of the individual as a whole occurs not alone in injury and fear, but also, though not so markedly, as a result of other phylogenetic associations, such as those of the chase and procreation. When adequate stimuli are repeated with such rapidity that the new stimulus is received before the effect of the previous one has worn off, a higher maximum effect is produced than is possible under a single stimulus, however powerful.

Sexual receptors are implanted in the body by natural selection, and the adequate stimuli excite the nerve-muscular reactions of conjugation in a manner analogous to the action of the adequate stimuli of the nociceptors. The specific response of either the sexual receptors or the nociceptors is at the expense of the total amount of nervous energy available at the moment. Likewise in daily labor, which, in the language of evolution, is the chase, nervous energy is expended. Under the dominance of fear or injury, however, the integration is most nearly absolute and probably every expenditure of nervous energy which is not required for efforts toward self-preservation is arrested; hence fear and injury drain the cup of energy to the dregs. This is the potential difference between fear and desire, between injury and conjugation.

What is the practical application of this? In operative surgery there is introduced a new principle, which removes from surgery much of the immediate risk from its trauma by establishing *anoci-association;* it places certain of the phenomena of fear on a physical basis; it explains to us the physical basis for the impairment of the entire individual under worry or misfortune; it makes evident the physical results of the daily noci-associations experienced by the individual as a social unit. On the other hand, it explains the power of therapeutic suggestion and of other influences which serve for the time to change the noci-integration; it shows the physical basis for the difference between hope and despair; it explains some of the phenomena of Graves' disease, of sexual neurasthenia, possibly of hay-fever and of the common cold.   The principle is probably equally applicable to the acute infections, in each of which chemical noci-association gives rise to many of the phenomena of the disease and it explains their cure by natural immunity and by vaccines.   This hypothesis should teach us to view our patients as a whole; and especially should it teach the surgeon gentleness.   It should teach us that there is something more in surgery than mechanics, and something more in medicine than physical diagnosis and drugs.

Conclusion

The brain-cells have existed for eons and, amid the vicissitudes of change, they have persisted with perhaps less alteration than has the crust of the earth.   Whether in man or in the lower animals, they are related to and obey the same general biologic laws, thus being bound to the entire past and performing their function in accordance with the law of phylogenetic association.

For so long a time have we directed our attention to tumors, infections, and injuries that we have not sufficiently considered the vital force itself.   We have viewed each anatomic and pathologic part as an entity and man as an isolated phenomenon in nature.   May we not find in the laws of adaptation under natural selection, and of phylogenetic association, the master key that will disclose to us the explanation of many pathologic phenomena as they have already explained many normal phenomena?

And may medicine not correlate the pathologic phenomena of the sick man with the forces of evolution, as the naturalists have correlated the phenomena of the sound man, and thus may not disease, as well as health, be given its evolutionary setting?

PHYLOGENETIC ASSOCIATION IN RELATION TO THE EMOTIONS *

The surgeon is familiar with the manifestations of every variety of the human emotions in the various stations of life, from infancy to senility, in health and in disease. Not only does he come into intimate contact with the emotions displayed by the victims of disease and of accidents, but he also observes those manifested by the relatives and friends of the families of his patients. Moreover, he is unhappily forced to notice the emotional effect upon himself when he is waging an unequal battle against death—the strain and worry at a crisis, when a life is in the balance and a single false move may be fatal, is an experience known only to the operating surgeon.

For the data for this paper, therefore, in which I shall for the most part limit my discussion to the strongest of all emotions—*fear*—I have drawn largely from my personal experience as a surgeon, as well as from an experimental research in which I have had the valuable assistance of my associates, Dr. H. G. Sloan, Dr. J. B. Austin, and Dr. M. L. Menten.

I believe it can be shown that it is possible to elicit the emotion of fear only in those animals that utilize a motor mechanism in defense against danger or in escape from it. For example, the defense of the skunk is a diabolic odor which repels its enemies; the skunk has no adequate equip-

* Address before the American Philosophical Society, Philadelphia, April 22, 1911.

ment for defense or escape by muscular exertion, and the skunk therefore shows little or no fear. Again, certain species of snakes are protected by venom; they possess no other means of defense nor have they adequate motor mechanisms for escape and they show no fear. Because of their strength other animals, such as the lion, the grizzly bear, and the elephant, show but little fear (Fig. 6). Animals which have an armored protection, such as the turtle, show little fear. It is, therefore, obvious that fear is not universal and that the emotion of fear is felt only by those animals whose self-preservation is dependent upon an uncertain adequacy of their power of muscular exertion either for defense or for flight (Fig. 7).

What are the principal phenomena of fear? They are palpitation of the heart, acceleration of the rate and alteration of the rhythm of the respiration, cold sweat, rise in body temperature, tremor, pallor, erection of the hair, suspension of the principal functions of digestion, muscular relaxation, and staring of the eyes (Fig. 12). The functions of the brain are wholly suspended except those which relate to the self-protective response against the feared object. Neither the brain nor any other organ of the body can respond to any other lesser stimulus during the dominance of fear.

From these premises it would appear that under the influence of fear, most, perhaps all, of the organs of the body are divided sharply into two classes: First, those that are stimulated, and, second, those that are inhibited. Those that are stimulated are the entire muscular system, the vasomotor and locomotor systems, the senses of perception, the respiration, the mechanism for erecting the hair, the sweat-glands, the thyroid gland, the adrenal gland (Cannon), and the special senses. On the other hand, all the digestive and procreative functions are inhibited. What is the significance of this stimulation of some and inhibition of other organs? As far as we know, the stimulated organs increase the efficiency of the animal for fight or for flight. It is through skeletal muscles that the physical attack or escape is effected; these muscles alone energize the claws, the teeth, the hoofs, and the means for flight. The increased action of the muscles of the heart and the blood-vessels increases the efficiency of the circulation; the secretion of the adrenal gland causes a rise in the blood-pressure; the increased action of the thyroid gland causes an increased metabolic activity; there is evidence that glycogen is actively called out, this being the most immediately available substance for the production of energy; the increased activity of the respiration is needed to supply the greater need of oxygen and the elimination of the increased amount of waste products; the dilatation of the nostrils affords a freer intake of air; the increased activity of the sweat-glands is needed to regulate the temperature of the body which the increased metabolism causes to rise. The activity of all the organs of perception—sight, hearing, smell—is increased in order that the danger may be more accurately perceived. It cannot be a mere coincidence that the organs and the tissues that are stimulated in the emotion of fear are precisely those that are actually utilized in a physical struggle for self-preservation.

Are any other organs stimulated by fear except those that can or that do assist in making a defensive struggle? I know of none. On the other hand, if an animal could dispense with his bulky digestive organs, whose functions are sus-

pended by fear, if he could, so to speak, clear his decks for
battle, it would be to his advantage.   Although the marvelous versatility of natural selection apparently could devise

FIG. 18.—DYING TIGER AT BAY.
"Fear is a phylogenetic fight or flight."   (Photo by Underwood and Underwood, N. Y.)

no means of affording this advantage, it nevertheless shut
off the nervous current and saved the vital force which is
ordinarily consumed by these non-combatants in the performance of their functions.   Whatever may be the origin

of fear, its phenomena are due to a stimulation of all the organs and tissues that add to the efficiency of the physical struggle for self-preservation and an inhibition of the func-

FIG. 19.—THE BROAD JUMP.
Note the similarity of the expression to the facial expression of fear and of anger (Figs. 12 and 21).   (Wm. J. Brownlow, drawn from photo.)

tions of the leading organs that do not participate in that struggle—the non-combatants, so to speak.

Fear arose from injury, and is one of the oldest and surely the strongest emotion.   By the slow process of vast empiricism nature has evolved the wonderful defensive motor me-

chanism of many animals and of man.   The stimulation of
this mechanism leading to a physical struggle is action, and
the stimulation of this mechanism without action is emotion.
We may say, therefore, that fear is a *phylogenetic fight or
flight* (Fig. 18).   On this hypothesis all the organs and parts

FIG. 20.—FINISH OF RELAY RACE.
Compare the facial expression of the runners with those in Figs. 12, 19, 22.
These pictures illustrate the fact that the same mechanism is stimulated
in emotion as in physical action.   (Photo by Underwood and Underwood,
N. Y.)

of the body are integrated, connected, or correlated for
the self-preservation of the individual by the activity of his
motor mechanism (Figs. 12, 19, and 20).   We fear not in our
hearts alone, not in our brains alone, not in our viscera
alone—fear influences every organ and tissue; each organ

or tissue is stimulated or inhibited according to its use or hindrance in the physical struggle for existence. By thus concentrating all or most of the nerve force on the nerve-muscular mechanism for defense, a greater physical power is developed. Hence it is that under the stimulus of fear animals are able to perform preternatural feats of strength. For the same reason, the exhaustion following fear will be increased as the powerful stimulus of fear drains the cup of nervous energy even though no visible action may result. An animal under the stimulus of fear may be likened to an automobile with the clutch thrown out but whose engine is racing at full speed. The gasoline is being consumed, the machinery is being worn, but the machine as a whole does not move, though the power of its engine may cause it to tremble.

When this conception is applied to the human beings of today, certain mysterious phenomena are at once elucidated. It must be borne in mind that man has not been presented with any new organs to meet the requirements of his present state of civilization; indeed, not only does he possess organs of the same type as those of his savage fellows, but of the same type also as those possessed by the lower animals even. In fact, man has reached his present status of civilization with the primary equipment of brutish organs. Perhaps the most striking difference between man and animals lies in the greater control which man has gained over his primitive instinctive reactions. As compared with the entire duration of organic evolution, man came down from his arboreal abode and assumed his new rôle of increased domination over the physical world but a moment ago. And now, though sitting at his desk in command of the complicated machinery of civilization, when he fears a business catastrophe his fear is manifested in the terms of his ancestral physical battle in the struggle for existence. He cannot fear intellectually, he cannot fear dispassionately, he fears with all his organs, and the same organs are stimulated and inhibited as if, instead of it being a battle of credit, of position, or of honor, it were a physical battle with teeth and claws. Whether the cause of acute fear be moral, financial, social, or stage fright, the heart beats wildly, the respirations are accelerated, perspiration is increased, there are pallor, trembling, indigestion, dry mouth, etc. The phenomena are those which accompany physical exertion in self-defense or escape. There is not one group of phenomena for the acute fear of the president of a bank in a financial crash and another for the hitherto trusted official who suddenly and unexpectedly faces the imminent probability of the penitentiary; or one for a patient who unexpectedly finds he has a cancer and another for the hunter when he shoots his first big game. Nature has but one means of response to fear, and whatever its cause the phenomena are always the same —always physical.

If the stimulus of fear be repeated from day to day, whether in the case of a mother anxious on account of the illness of a child; a business man struggling against failure; a politician under contest for appointment; a broker in the daily hazard of his fortune; litigants in legal battle, or a jealous lover who fears a rival; the countless real as well as the baseless fears in daily life, in fact, all forms of fear, as it seems to me, express themselves in like terms of ancestral physical contests. On this law, fear dominates the various organs and parts of the body.

Anger and fear express opposite emotional states. Fear is the expression of a strong desire to escape from danger; anger, of a strong desire to attack physically and to vanquish opposition. This hypothesis is strongly supported by the outward expressions of fear and of anger. When the busi-

FIG. 21.—ANGRY CAT PREPARED TO FIGHT.

ness man is conducting a struggle for existence against his rivals, and when the contest is at its height, he may clench his fists, pound the table, perhaps show his teeth, and exhibit every expression of physical combat. Fixing the jaw and showing the teeth in anger merely emphasize the remarkable tenacity of phylogeny. Although the development of the wonderful efficiency of the hands has led to a modification of the once powerful canines of our progenitors, the ancestral use of the teeth for attack and defense is attested in the display of anger. In all stations of life differences of opinion may lead to argument and argument to physical combats, even to the point of killing. The physical violence of the savage and of the brute still lies surprisingly near the surface (Fig. 21).

We have now presented some of the reasons based largely on gross animal behavior why fear is to be regarded as a response to phylogenetic association with physical danger. In further support of this hypothesis, I shall now present some clinical and experimental evidence. Although there is not convincing proof, yet there is evidence that the effect of the stimulus of fear upon the body when unaccompanied by physical activity is more injurious than is an actual physical contest which results in fatigue without gross physical injury. It is well known that the soldier who, while under fire, waits in vain for orders to charge, suffers more than the soldier who flings himself into the fray; and that a wild animal endeavoring to avoid capture suffers less than one cowering in captivity. An unexpressed smouldering emotion is measurably relieved by action. It is probable that the various energizing substances needed in physical combat, such as the secretions of the thyroid, the adrenals (Cannon), etc., may cause physical injury to the body when they are not consumed by action (Fig. 22).

That the brain is definitely influenced—damaged even—by fear has been proved by the following experiments: Rabbits were frightened by a dog but were neither injured nor chased. After various periods of time the animals were killed and their brain-cells compared with the brain-cells of normal animals—wide-spread changes were seen (Fig. 13). The principal clinical phenomena expressed by the rabbit were

Fig. 22.—The damaging effects of the emotions of which this woman has been the victim—whether fear or anger, or both—are plainly evident in the pallid face and the typical facies of intense exhaustion. (Photo by Brown Bros., N. Y.)

rapid heart, accelerated respiration, prostration, tremors, and a rise in temperature. The dog showed similar phenomena, excepting that, instead of such muscular relaxation as was shown by the rabbit, it exhibited aggressive muscular action. Both the dog and the rabbit were exhausted but, although the dog exerted himself actively and the rabbit remained physically passive, the rabbit was much more exhausted.

Further observations were made upon the brain of a fox which had been chased for two hours by members of a hunt club, and had been finally overtaken by the hounds and killed. Most of the brain-cells of this fox, as compared with those of a normal fox, showed extensive physical changes (Fig. 4).

The next line of evidence is offered with some reservation, but it has seemed to me to be more than mere idle speculation. It relates to the phenomena of one of the most interesting diseases in the entire category of human ailments— I refer to exophthalmic goiter, or Graves' disease, a disease primarily involving the emotions. This disease is frequently the direct sequence of severe mental shock or of a long and intensely worrying strain. The following case is typical: A broker was in his usual health up to the panic of 1907; during this panic his fortune and that of others were for almost a year in jeopardy, failure finally occurring. During this heavy strain he became increasingly nervous and by imperceptible degrees there developed a pulsating enlargement of the thyroid gland, an increased prominence of the eyes, marked increase in perspiration—profuse sweating even—palpitation of the heart, increased respiration with frequent sighing, increase in blood-pressure; there were tremor of many muscles, rapid loss of weight and strength, frequent gastro-intestinal disturbances, loss of normal control of his emotions, and marked impairment of his mental faculties. He was as completely broken in health as in fortune. These phenomena resembled closely those of fear and followed in the wake of a strain which was due to fear.

In young women exophthalmic goiter often follows in the wake of a disappointment in love; in women, too, it frequently follows the illnesses of children or parents during which they have had to endure the double strain of worry and of constant care. Since such strains usually fall most heavily upon women, they are the most frequent victims of this disease. Now, whatever the exciting cause of exophthalmic goiter, whether it be unusual business worry, disappointment in love, a tragedy, or the illness of a loved one, the symptoms are alike and closely resemble the phenomena of one of the great primitive emotions. How could disappointment in love play a rôle in the causation of Graves' disease? If the hypothesis which has been presented as an explanation of the genesis and the phenomena of fear be correct, then that hypothesis explains also the emotion of love. If fear be a phylogenetic physical defense or escape which does not result in muscular action, then love is a phylogenetic conjugation without physical action. The quickened pulse, the leaping heart, the accelerated respiration, the sighing, the glowing eye, the crimson cheek, and many other phenomena are merely phylogenetic recapitulations of ancestral acts. The thyroid gland is believed to participate in such physical activities. Hence it may well follow that the disappointed maiden who is intensely integrated for a youth will, at every thought of him, be subjected by phylogenetic association to a specific stimulation analogous to that which attended the ancestral consummation. Moreover, a happy marriage has many times been followed by a cure of the exophthalmic goiter which appeared in the wake of such an experience.

The victims of Graves' disease present a counterpart of emotional exhaustion. That the emotions in Graves' disease are abnormally acute is illustrated by my personal observation of the death of a subject of this disease from fear alone. Whatever the exciting cause of this disease, the symptoms are the same; just as in fear, the phenomena are the same whatever the exciting cause.

Figures 12 and 16 show the resemblance between the outward appearances of a patient with Graves' disease and of a person obsessed by fear. Fear and Graves' disease have the following phenomena in common: Increased heart-beat, increased respiration, rising temperature, muscular tremors, protruding eyes, loss in weight; Cannon has found an increased amount of adrenalin in the blood in fear and Frankel in Graves' disease; increased blood-pressure; muscular weakness; digestive disturbances; impaired nervous control; hypersusceptibility to stimuli; in protracted intense fear the brain-cells show marked physical changes, and in Graves' disease analogous changes are seen (Figs. 13 C and 15). In Graves' disease there seems to be a composite picture of an intense expression of the great primitive emotions. If Graves' disease be a disease of the great primitive emotions, or rather of the whole motor mechanism, how is the constant flow of stimulation of this complicated mechanism supplied? It would seem that there must be secreted in excessive amount some substance that activates the motor mechanism. The nervous system in Graves' disease is hypersusceptible to stimuli and to thyroid extract. It might follow that even a normal amount of thyroid secretion would lead to excessive stimulation of the hypersusceptible motor mechanism.

This condition of excessive motor activity and hyper-excitability may endure for years. What is the source of this pathologic excitation? The following facts may give a clue. In suitable cases of Graves' disease, if the thyroid secretion is sufficiently diminished by a removal of a part of the gland or by interrupting the nerve and the blood supply, the phenomena of the disease áre diminished immediately, and in favorable cases the patient is restored to approximately the normal condition. The heart action slows, the respiratory rate falls, the restlessness diminishes, digestive disturbances disappear, tremors decrease, there is a rapid increase in the body weight, and the patient gradually resumes his normal state. On the other hand, if for a period of time extract of the thyroid gland is administered to a *normal* individual in excessive dosage, there will develop nervousness, palpitation of the heart, sweating, loss of weight, slight protrusion of the eyes, indigestion; in short, most of the phenomena of Graves' disease and of the strong emotions will be produced artificially (Figs. 15 and 23). When the administration of the thyroid extract is discontinued, these phenomena may disappear. On the other hand, when there is too little or no thyroid gland, the individual becomes dull, stupid, and emotionless, though he may be irritable; while if a sufficient amount of thyroid extract be given to such a patient he may be brought back to his normal condition.

Hence we see that the phenomena of the emotions may within certain limits be increased, diminished, or abolished by increasing, diminishing, or totally excluding the secretion of the thyroid gland.

Graves' disease may be increased by giving thyroid extract and by fear. It may be diminished by removing a part of the gland, or by interrupting the blood and nerve supply, or by complete rest. In addition, at some stage of Graves' disease there is an increase in the size and in the number of the secreting cells. These facts regarding the normal and the pathologic supply of thyroid secretion point to this gland as one of the sources of the energizing substance or substances, by means of which the motor phenomena of animals are executed and their emotions expressed.

Anger is similar to fear in origin and, like fear, is an integration and stimulation of the motor mechanism and its accessories. Animals which have no natural weapons for attack experience neither fear nor anger, while the animals which have weapons for attack express anger principally by energizing the muscles used in attack. Although, as has already been stated, the efficiency of the hands of man has largely supplanted the use of the teeth, he still shows his teeth in anger and so gives support to the theory that this emotion is of remote ancestral origin and proves the great persistence of phylogenetic association. On this conception we can understand why it is that a patient consumed by worry—which to me signifies interrupted stimulation, a state of alternation between hope and fear—suffers so many bodily impairments and diseases even. This hypothesis explains the slow dying of animals in captivity. It explains the grave digestive and metabolic disturbances which appear under any nerve strain, especially under the strain of fear,

Fig. 23.

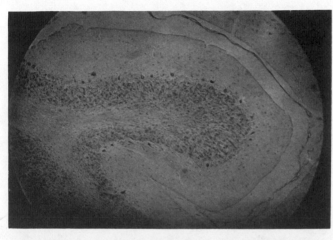

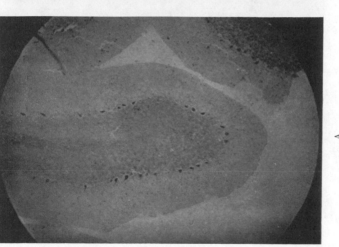

A

SECTION OF CEREBELLUM OF DOG—NORMAL (× 85).

B

SECTION OF CEREBELLUM OF A DOG SHOWING EFFECT OF THYROID FEEDING (× 85).

Compare with the photomicrograph in Fig. 15 and note the like evidence of the results of excessive activation of the system with thyroid, as shown by the loss of cytoplasm and the degeneration of the Purkinje cells.

and the great benefits of confidence and hope; it explains the nervousness, loss of weight, indigestion—in short, the comprehensive physical changes that are wrought by fear and by sexual love and hate. On this hypothesis we can understand the physical influence of one individual over the body and personality of another; and of the infinite factors in environment that, through phylogenetic association, play a rôle in the functions of many of our organs. It is because under the uncompromising law of survival of the fittest we were evolved as motor beings that we do not possess any organs or faculties which have not served our progenitors in accomplishing their survival in the relentless struggle of organic forms with one another. We are now, as we were then, essentially motor beings, and the only way in which we can meet the dangers in our environment is by a motor response. Such a motor response implies the integration of our entire being for action, this integration involving the activity of certain glands, such as the adrenals (Cannon), the thyroid, the liver, etc., which throw into the blood-stream substances which help to form energy, but which, if no muscular action ensues, are harmful elements in the blood. While this motor preparation is going on, the entire digestive tract is inhibited. It thus becomes clear why an emotion is more harmful than action.

Any agency that can sufficiently inspire faith,—dispel worry,—whether that agency be mystical, human, or divine, will at once stop the body-wide stimulations and inhibitions which cause lesions which are as truly physical as is a fracture. The striking benefits of good luck, success, and happiness; of a change of scene; of hunting and fishing; of optimistic and helpful friends, are at once explained by this

hypothesis. One can also understand the difference between the broken body and spirits of an animal in captivity
and its buoyant return to its normal condition when freed.

But time will not permit me to follow this tempting lead,
which has been introduced for another purpose—the proposal of a remedy.

Worries either are or are not groundless. Of those that
have a basis, many are exaggerated. It has occurred to me
to utilize as an antidote an appeal to the same great law that
originally excited the instinctive involuntary reaction known
as fear—the law of self-preservation.

I have found that if an intelligent patient who is suffering
from fear can be made to see so plainly as to become firmly
convinced that his brain, his various organs, indeed his whole
being, could be physically damaged by fear, that this same
instinct of self-preservation will, to the extent of his con-
viction, banish fear. It is hurling a threatened active mil-
itant danger, whose injurious influences are both certain
and known, against an uncertain, perhaps a fancied, one. In
other words, fear itself is an injury which when recognized
is instinctively avoided. In a similar manner anger may be
softened or banished by an appeal to the stronger self-
preserving instinct aroused by the fear of physical damage,
such as the physical injury of brain-cells. This playing of
one primitive instinct against another is comparable to the
effect produced upon two men who are quarreling when a
more powerful enemy of both comes threateningly on the
scene.

The acute fear of a surgical operation may be banished
by the use of certain drugs that depress the associational
power of the brain and so minimize the effect of the prepara-

tions that usually inspire fear. If, in addition, the entire field of operation is blocked by local anesthesia so that the associational centers are not awakened, the patient will pass through the operation unscathed.

The phylogenetic origin of fear is injury, hence injury and fear cause the same phenomena. In their quality and in their phenomena psychic shock and traumatic shock are the same. The perception of danger by the special senses in the sound of the opening gun of a battle, or in the sight of a venomous snake, is phylogenetically the same and causes the same effects upon the entire body as an operation under anesthesia or a physical combat in that each drives the motor mechanism. The use of local anesthetics in the operative field prevents nerve-currents from the seat of injury from reaching the brain and there integrating the entire body for a self-defensive struggle. The result, even though a part of the brain is asleep and the muscles paralyzed, is the same as that produced by the interception of the terri-fying sound of the gun, or of the sight of the dangerous reptile, since the stimulation of the motor mechanism is prevented.

By both the positive and the negative evidence we are forced to believe that the emotions are primitive instinctive reactions which represent ancestral acts; and that they there-fore utilize the complicated motor mechanism which has been developed by the forces of evolution as that best adapted to fit the individual for his struggle with his environment or for procreation.

The mechanism by which the motor acts are performed and the mechanism by which the emotions are expressed are one and the same.   These acts in their infinite complexity are suggested by association—phylogenetic association. When our progenitors came in contact with any exciting element in their environment, action ensued then and there. There was much action—little restraint or emotion. Civilized man is really in auto-captivity. He is subjected to innumerable stimulations, but custom and convention frequently prevent physical action. When these stimulations are sufficiently strong but no action ensues, the reaction constitutes an emotion. A phylogenetic fight is anger; a phylogenetic flight is fear; a phylogenetic copulation is sexual love, and so one finds in this conception an underlying principle which may be the key to an understanding of the emotions and of certain diseases.

FEAR, ANGER, LOVE

PAIN, LAUGHTER, AND CRYING*

PAIN

Pain, like other phenomena, was probably evolved for a particular purpose—surely for the good of the individual; like fear and worry, it frequently is injurious. What then may be its purpose?

We postulate that pain is one of the phenomena which result from a stimulation to motor action. When a barefoot boy steps on a sharp stone it is important that the injuring contact be released as quickly as possible; and therefore physical injury pain results and impels the required action. Anemia of the soft parts at the points of pressure results from prolonged sitting or lying in one position, and as a result pain compels a muscular action that shifts the damaging pressure—this is the pain of anemia; when the rays of the blazing sun shine directly upon the retina, pain immediately causes a protective muscular action—the lid is closed, the head turns away—this is light pain; when standing too close to a blazing fire the excessive heat causes a pain which results in the protective muscular action of moving away—this is heat pain; when the urinary bladder is acutely overdistended the resultant pain induces voluntary as well as involuntary muscular contraction—this is evacuation pain; associated with defecation is a characteristic warning pain, and an active pain which induces the required muscular action—this, like the pain accompanying

* Address delivered before the John Ashhurst, Jr., Surgical Society of the University of Pennsylvania, May 3, 1912.

micturition, is an evacuation pain; in obstruction of the urinary passages and of the large and the small intestine the pain is exaggerated, as is the accompanying muscular contraction—this is a pathologic evacuation pain; when the fetus reaches full term and labor is to begin, it is heralded by pain which is associated with rhythmic contractions of the uterine muscle; later, many other muscles take part in the birth and pain is associated with all these muscular contractions—these are labor pains; when a foreign body, be it ever so small, falls upon the conjunctiva or cornea there results what is perhaps the acutest pain known, and quick and active muscular action follows—this is special contact pain. Special pain receptors are placed in certain parts of the nose, the pharynx, and the larynx, the stimulation of which causes special motor acts, such as sneezing, hawking, coughing. Curiously vague pains are associated with the protective motor act of vomiting and with the sexual motor acts—these may be termed nausea pains and pleasure pains. We now see, therefore, that against the injurious physical contacts of environment, against heat and cold, against damaging sunlight, against local anemia when resting or sleeping, the body is protected by virtue of the muscular action which results from pain. Then, too, for the emptying of the pregnant uterus, for the evacuation of the intestine and of the urinary bladder as normal acts, and for the overcoming of obstructions in these tracts, pain compels the required muscular actions. For passing gall-stones and urinary calculi, urgent motor stimuli are awakened by pain. For each of these diversified pains the consequent muscular action is specific in type, distribution, and intensity. This statement is so commonplace that we are apt to miss the significance and the wonder of it. It is probable that every nerve-ending in the skin and every type of stimulation represents a separate motor pattern, the adequate stimulation of which causes always the same response.

Let us pass on to the discussion of another and perhaps even more interesting type of pain, that associated with infection. Not all kinds of infection are painful; and in those infections that may be associated with pain there is pain only when certain regions of the body are involved. Among the infections that are not associated with pain are scarlet fever, typhoid fever, measles, malaria, whooping-cough, typhus fever, and syphilis in its early stages. The infections that are usually, though not always, associated with pain are the pyogenic infections. The pyogenic infections and the exanthemata constitute the great majority of infections and are the basis of the discussion which follows.

I will state one of my principal conclusions first, i. e., that the only types of infection that are associated with pain are those in which the infection may be spread by muscular action or those in which the fixation of parts by continued muscular rigidity is an advantage; and, further, as a striking corollary, that the type of infection that may cause muscular action when it attacks one region of the body may cause no such action when it attacks another region.

The primary, and perhaps the most striking, difference between the painless exanthemata and the painful pyogenic infections is that in the case of the exanthemata the protective response of the body is a chemical one,—-the formation of antibodies in the blood, which usually produce permanent immunity,—while the response to the pyogenic infections is largely phagocytic. In the pyogenic infections, in order to protect the remainder of the body, which, of course, enjoys no immunity, every possible barrier against the spread of the infection is thrown about the local point of infection. How are these barriers formed? First, lymph is poured out, then the part is fixed by the continuous contraction of the neighboring muscles and by the inhibition of those muscles that, in the course of their ordinary function, would by their contractions spread the infection. Wherever there is protective muscular rigidity there is also pain. On the other hand, in pyogenic infections in the substance of the liver, in the substance of the kidney, within the brain, in the retroperitoneal space, in the lobes of the lung, in the chambers of the heart and in the blood-vessels of the chest and the abdomen, in all locations in which muscular contractions can in no way assist in localizing the disease, pyogenic infections produce no muscular rigidity and no pain. Apparently, therefore, only those infections are painful which are associated with a protective muscular contraction. This explains why tuberculosis of the hip is painful, while tuberculosis of the lung is painless.

There is a third type of pain which modifies muscular action in a curious way. We have already stated that local pain serves an adaptive purpose. In this light let us now consider headache. Headache is one of the commonest initiatory symptoms of the various infections, especially of those infections which are accompanied by no local pain and by no local muscular action. In peritonitis, cholecystitis, pleurisy, arthritis, appendicitis, salpingitis, child-birth, in obstructions of the intestinal and the genito-urinary tract, in short, in those acute processes in which the local symptoms are powerful enough to govern the individual as a whole,—

to make him lie down and keep quiet, refuse food and possibly reject what is already in the stomach,—in all these conditions there is rarely a headache, but in the diseases in which local pain is absent, such as the exanthemata, typhoid fever, and auto-intoxication, which have no dominating local disturbances to act as policemen to put the individual to bed and to make him refuse food that he may be in the most favorable position to combat the oncoming disease, in such cases in which these masterful and beneficent local influences are absent we postulate that headache has been evolved to perform this important service.

On the hypothesis that it is good for the individual who is acutely stricken by a disease or who is poisoned by auto-intoxication to rest and fast, and that the muscular system obeys the imperial command of pain, and in view of the fact that the brain is not only in constant touch with the conditions of every part of the body but that it is also the controlling organ of the body, one would expect that in these diseases the major pain whose purpose it is to govern general muscular action would be located in the head and there we find it. How curious and yet how intelligible is the fact that, though a headache may be induced by even a slight auto-intoxication, an abscess may exist within the brain without causing pain. When an obliterative endarteritis is threatening a leg with anemic gangrene, or when one lies too long in the same position on a hard bed, there is threatening injury from local anemia, and as a result there is acute pain, but when the obliterative endarteritis threatens anemia of the brain, or when an embolism or thrombosis has produced anemia of the brain, there may be no accompanying pain. The probable explanation of the pain which results

6

in the first instance and the lack of pain in the second is that
in the former muscular action constitutes a self-protective
response, but in the other it does not.   Diseases and injuries of the brain are notoriously difficult to diagnosticate.
This may well be because it has always been so well protected by the skull that there have been evolved within it
few tell-tale self-protective responses, so that in the presence
of injury and disease within itself the brain remains remarkably silent.   It should occasion no surprise that there are in
the brain no receptors, the mechanical stimulation of which
can cause pain, because its bony covering has always prevented the adaptive implantation within it of contact pain
receptors.   Dr. Frazier tells me that in the course of his
operations on the brains of unanesthetized patients he is
able to explore the entire brain freely and without pain.
From my own experience I am able to confirm Dr. Frazier's
observation.   In addition, the two-stage operation for the
excision of the Gasserian ganglion provides an observation
of extraordinary interest.   If at the first séance the ganglion
is exposed, but is not disturbed except by the iodoform gauze
packing, then on the following day the gauze may be removed, the ganglion picked up, and its branches and root
excised without anesthesia and without pain.   The same
statement and explanation may be made regarding the distribution of pain receptors for physical contact within the
parenchyma of the liver, the gall-bladder, the abdominal
viscera, the spleen, the heart, the lungs, the retroperitoneal
tissue, the deep tissue of the back, the vertebræ, and in
certain portions of the spinal cord.   Just what is the distribution of the receptors for heat and for cold I am unable
to state, but this much we do know, that without anesthesia

the intestines may be cauterized freely without the least pain resulting, and in animals the cauterization of the brain causes no demonstrable change in the circulatory or respiratory reactions. It is probable therefore that the distribution of the pain receptors for physical contact and for heat are limited to those parts of the body that have been exposed to injurious contacts with environment.

Of special significance is the pain which is due to cold, which increases muscular tone and produces shivering. The general increase in muscular tone produces an interesting postural phenomenon: the limbs are flexed and the body bent forward, a position which probably is due to the fact that the flexors are stronger than the extensors. As muscular action is always accompanied by heat production, the purpose of the muscular contraction and the shivering is quite certainly caused by cold to assist in the maintenance of the normal body temperature.

We have now discussed many of the causes of pain and in each instance we have found an associated muscular action which apparently serves some adaptive purpose (Figs. 24 and 25). If we assume that pain exists for the purpose of stimulating muscular reactions, we may well inquire what part of the nervous arc is the site of the sensation of pain—the nerve-endings, the trunk, or the brain? Does pain result from physical contact with the nerve-endings, with the physical act of transmitting an impression along the nerve trunk, or with the process within the brain-cells by which energy is released to cause a motor act?

It seems most probable that the site of the pain is in the brain-cells. If this be so, then what is the physical process by which the phenomena of pain are produced? The one

FIG. 24.—THE LAOCOÖN.
The muscular activation and facies of the father most strikingly illustrate the
physical expression of pain.

hypothesis that can be tested experimentally is that pain is
a phenomenon resulting from the rapid discharge of energy
in the brain-cells.   If this be true, then if every pain receptor
of the body were equally stimulated in such a manner that

FIG. 25.—FEAR AND AGONY.
"Amid this dread exuberance of woe ran naked spirits wing'd with horrid
fear."—Dante's "Inferno," Canto XXIV, lines 89, 90.

all the stimuli reached the brain-cells simultaneously, the
cells would find themselves in equilibrium and no motor act
would be performed.   But if all the pain receptors of the
body but one were equally stimulated, and this one stimu-

lated harder than the rest, then the latter would gain possession of the final common path, the sensation of pain would be felt, and a muscular contraction would result.

It is well known that when a greater pain is thrown into competition with a lesser one, the lesser is completely submerged. In this manner the school-boy initiates the novice into the mystery of the painless plucking of hair. The simultaneous, but severe application of the boot to the blindfolded victim takes complete and exclusive possession of the final common path and the hair is painlessly plucked through the triumph of the boot stimulus over the hair stimulus in the struggle for the possession of the final common path.

Another argument in favor of this hypothesis that pain is an accompaniment of the release of energy in the brain-cells is found in the fact that painless stimuli received through the special senses may completely submerge the painful stimuli of physical injury; for although the stimuli to motor action, which are received through the senses of sight, hearing, and smell, cause even more powerful motor action than those caused by physical contact stimuli, yet they are not accompanied by pain. Examples of this triumph of stimulation of the special senses over contact stimulation are frequently seen in persons obsessed by anger or fear, and to a less degree in those obsessed by sexual emotion. In the fury of battle the soldier may not perceive his wound until the emotional excitation is wearing away, when the sensation of warm blood on the skin may first attract his attention. Religious fanatics are said to feel no pain when they subject themselves to self-injury. Now, since both psychic and mechanical stimuli cause motor action by the excitation of precisely the same mechanism in the brain, and since the more rapid release of energy from psychic stimuli submerges the physical stimuli and prevents pain, it would seem that pain must be a phenomenon which is associated with the process of releasing energy by the brain-cells. Were physical injury inflicted in a quiescent state equal to that inflicted in the emotional state, great pain and intense muscular action would be experienced. Now the emotions are as purely motor excitants as is pain. The dynamic result is the same, the principal difference being the greater suddenness and the absolute specificity of the pain stimuli as compared with the more complex and less peremptory stimuli of the emotions. A further evidence that pain is a product of the release of brain-cell energy is the probability that if one could pierce the skin at many points on a limb in such a manner that antagonistic points only were equally and simultaneously stimulated, then an equilibrium in the governing brain-cells would be established and neither pain nor motion would follow. An absolute test of this assumption cannot be made but it is supported by the obtainable evidence.

We will now turn to a new viewpoint, a practical as well as a fascinating one, which can best be illustrated by two case histories: A man, seventy-eight years old, whose chief complaint was obstinate constipation, was admitted to the medical ward of the Lakeside Hospital several years ago. The abdomen was but slightly distended; there was no fever, no increased leukocytosis, no muscular rigidity, and but slight general tenderness. He claimed to have lost in weight and strength during the several months previous to his admission. A tentative diagnosis of malignant tumor of the large intestine was made, but free movements were secured rather easily, and we abandoned the idea of an exploratory operation. The patient gradually failed and died without a definite diagnosis having been made by either the medical or the surgical service. At autopsy there was found a wide-spread peritonitis arising from a perforated appendix.

A child, several years old, was taken ill with some indefinite disease. A number of the ablest medical and surgical consultants of a leading medical center thoroughly and repeatedly investigated the case. Although they could make no definite diagnosis they all agreed that the trouble surely could not be appendicitis because there was neither muscular rigidity nor tenderness. The autopsy showed a gangrenous appendix and general peritonitis.

How can these apparently anomalous cases be explained? These two cases are illustrations of the same principle that underlies the freedom from pain which results from the use of narcotics and anesthetics, the same principle that explains the fact that cholecystitis may occur in the aged without any other local symptoms than the presence of a mass and perhaps very slight tenderness; and that accounts in general for the lack of well-expressed disease phenomena in senility and in infancy. The reason why the aged, the very young, and the subjects of general paresis show but few symptoms of disease is that in senility the brain is deteriorated, while in infancy the brain is so undeveloped that the mechanism of association is inactive, hence pain and tenderness, which are among the oldest of the associations, are wanting. Senility and infancy are by nature normally narcotized. The senile are passing through the twilight into the night; while infants are traversing through the dawn into the day. Hence it is that the diagnosis of injury and disease in the extremes of life is beset by especial difficulties, since the entire body is as silent as are the brain, the pericardium, the mediastinum, and other symptomless areas.

For the same reason, when a patient who is seriously ill with a painful disease turns upon the physician a glowing eye and an eager face, and remarks how comfortable he feels, then the end is near. This is a brilliant and fateful clinical mirage.

When one reflects on the vast amount of evidence as to the origin and the purpose of pain, he is forced to conclude that pain is a phenomenon of motor stimulation, and that its principal rôle is the protection of the individual against the gross and the microscopic enemies in his environment. The benefits of pain are especially manifested in the urgent muscular actions by means of which the body moves away from physical injury; obstructions of the hollow viscera are overcome; rest is compelled in the acute infections—the infected points are held rigidly quiet, the muscles of the abdomen are fixed, and harmful peristalsis is arrested in peritonitis; while there is absolutely no pain in the diseases or injuries which affect those regions of the body in which in the course of evolution no pain receptors were placed, or in those diseases in which muscular inhibition or contraction is of no help. In a biologic sense pain is closely associated with the emotional stimuli, for both pain and the emotions incite motor activity for the good of the individual.

The frequent occurrence of post-operative and post-traumatic pain is accounted for by the fact that the operation or the injury has lowered the threshold of the brain-cells to trauma; the brain and not the local sensitive field is the site of the pain. I have found that, by blocking the field of operation with local anesthesia, post-operative pain is diminished; that is, since the local anesthesia prevents the strong stimuli of the trauma from reaching the brain, its threshold is not lowered. There is a close resemblance between the phenomena of pain habit, of education, of physical training, of love and of hate. In education, in pain habit, in all emotional relations, a low brain-cell threshold is established which facilitates the reception of specific stimuli; all these processes are motor acts, or are symbolic of motor acts, and we may be trained to perceive misfortune and pain as readily as we are trained to perceive mathematical formulæ or moral precepts. In each and every case, readiness of perception depends, as it seems to me, upon a modified state of the brain-cells, their threshold especially, the final degree of perception possible in any individual being perhaps based on the type of potential molecules of which the brain is built. We must believe also that every impression is permanent, as only thus could an individual animal or a man be fitted by his own experience for life's battles.

LAUGHTER AND CRYING

What is laughter? What is its probable origin, its distribution, and its purpose?

Laughter is an involuntary rhythmic contraction of certain respiratory muscles, usually accompanied by certain vocal sounds. It is a motor act of the respiratory apparatus primarily, although if intense it may involve not only the extraordinary muscles of respiration, but most of the muscles of the body. There are many degrees of laughter, from the mere brightening of the eyes, a fleeting smile, tittering and giggling, to hysteric and convulsive laughter. Under certain circumstances, laughter may be so intense and so long continued that it leads to considerable exhaustion.

The formation of tears is sometimes associated with laughter. When integrated with laughter, the nervous system can perform no other function. Crying is closely associated with laughter, and in children especially laughter and crying are readily interchanged.

We postulate that laughter and weeping serve a useful purpose. According to Darwin, only man and monkeys laugh (Fig. 26); other animals exhibit certain types of facial expression accompanying various emotions, but laughter in the sense in which that word is commonly used is probably an attribute of the primates only, although it is probable that many animals find substitutes for laughter.

The proneness of man to laughter is modified by age, sex, training, mental state, health, and by many other factors. Healthy, happy children are especially prone to laughter, while disease, strong emotions, fatigue, and age diminish laughter. Women laugh more than do men. The healthy, happy maturing young woman perhaps laughs most, especially when she is slightly embarrassed.

What causes laughter? Good news, high spirits, tickling, hearing and seeing others laugh; droll stories; flashes of wit; passages of humor; averted injury; threatened breach of the conventions; and numerous other causes might be added. It is obvious that laughter may be produced by diverse influences, many of which are so unlike each other that it would at first sight seem improbable that a single general principle underlies all. Before presenting a hypothesis which harmonizes most of the facts, and which may offer an explanation of the origin and purpose of laughter, let us return for a moment to some previous considerations—that man is essentially a motor being; that all his responses to the physical forces of his environment are motor;

FIG. 26.—LAUGHING CHIMPANZEE.

"Mike," the clever chimpanzee in the London Zoo, evidently enjoys a joke as well as any one else. (Photo by Underwood and Underwood, N. Y.)

that thoughts and words even are symbolic of motor acts; that in the emotions of fear, of anger, and of sexual love the whole body is integrated for acts which are not performed. These integrations stimulate the brain-cells, the ductless glands, and other parts, and the energizing secretions, among which are epinephrin, thyroid and hypophyseal secretions, are thrown into the blood-stream, while that most available fuel, glycogen, is also mobilized in the blood. This body-wide preparation for action may be designated kinetic reaction. The fact that emotion is more injurious to the body than is muscular action is well known, the difference being probably caused by the fact that when there is action the above-mentioned products of stimulation are consumed, while in stimulation without action they are not consumed and must be eliminated as waste products. Now these activating substances and the fuel glycogen may be consumed by any muscular action as well as by the particular muscular action for which the integration and consequent stimulation were made; that is, if one were provoked to such anger that he felt impelled to attack the object of his anger, one of three things might happen: First, he might perform no physical act but give expression to the emotion of anger; second, he might engage in a physical struggle and completely satisfy his anger; third, he might immediately engage in violent gymnastic exercises and thus consume all the motor-producing elements mobilized by the anger and thus clarify his body.

In these premises we find our explanation of the origin and purpose of laughter and crying, for since they consist almost wholly of muscular exertion, they serve precisely such clarifying purposes as would be served by the gymnastic exercises of an angry man. As it seems to me, the muscular action of laughter clears the system of the energizing substances which have been mobilized in various parts of the body for the performance of other actions (Figs. 27 to 29). If this be true, the first question that presents itself is, Why

Fig. 27.—The facies of this freckle-faced boy is an excellent illustration of the expression in laughter of effervescent and infinitely varied possibilities of motor activity.

Fig. 28.—The snap-shot was taken without the subject's knowledge and discloses admirably the activation of the facial muscles which are associated with hearty laughter.

is the respiratory system utilized for such a clarifying purpose? Why do we not laugh with our feet and hands as
well? Were laughter expressed with the hands, the monkey
might fall from the tree and, if by the feet, man might fall
to the ground. He would at least be ataxic. In fact,
laughter has the great advantage of utilizing a group of
powerful muscles which can be readily spared without

FIG. 29.—The laughter of this boy is doubtless the outward physical expression of the motor activation excited by the anticipation of vigorous out-
door exercise. When he begins to exercise, this laughter will diminish or
disappear.

seriously interfering with the maintenance of posture.
Laughter, however, is only one form of muscular action which
may consume the fuel thrown into the blood by excitation.
That these products of excitation are often consumed by
other motor acts than laughter is frequently seen in public
meetings when the stamping of feet and the clapping of
hands in applause gives relief to the excitation (Fig. 30).

Fig. 30.—Happy Fans in the Bleachers after Three Doubles in the Fourth Inning of a Championship Game.

Note the laughter and muscular actions in which their excitation is finding relief. (Copyright by Underwood and Underwood, N. Y.)

Why the noise of laughter? In order that the products of excitation may be quickly and completely consumed, the powerful group of expiratory muscles must have some resistance against which they can exert themselves strongly and at the same time provide for adequate respiratory exchange. The intermittent closure of the epiglottis serves this purpose admirably, just as the horizontal bars afford the resistance against which muscles may be exercised. The facial muscles are not in use for other purposes, hence their contractions will consume a little of the fuel. An audience excited by the words of an impassioned speaker undergoes a body-wide stimulation for action, all of which may be eliminated by laughter or by applause (Fig. 31).

Let us test this hypothesis by some practical examples. The first is an incident that accidentally occurred in our laboratory during experiments on fear which were performed as follows: A keen, snappy fox terrier was completely muzzled by winding a broad strip of adhesive plaster around his jaw so as to include all but the nostrils. When this aggressive little terrier and the rabbit found themselves in close quarters each animal became completely governed by instinct; the rabbit crouched in fear, while the terrier, with all the ancestral assurance of seizing his prey, rushed upon the rabbit, his muzzle always glancing off and his attack ending in awkward failure.

This experiment was repeated many times and each time provoked the serious-minded scientific visitors who witnessed it to laughter. Why? Because the spectacle of a savage little terrier rushing upon an innocent rabbit as if to mangle it integrated the body of the onlooker with a strong desire to exert muscular action to prevent the cruelty. This

7

Fig. 31.—Spectators at Interscholastic Football Game.

Note how the body-wide stimulation caused by a successful play has stimulated each individual boy to action which is expressed in laughter and in general muscular activity. (Copyright by Underwood and Underwood, N. Y.)

integration caused a conversion of the potential energy in the brain-cells into kinetic energy, and there resulted a discharge into the blood-stream of activating internal secretions for the purpose of producing muscular action. Instantly and unexpectedly the danger passed and the preparation for muscular action intended for use in the protection of the rabbit was not needed. This fuel was consumed by the neutral muscular action of laughter, which thus afforded relief.

A common example of the same nature is that encountered on the street when a pedestrian slips on a banana peel and, just as he is about to tumble, recovers his equilibrium. The onlookers secure relief from the integration to run to his rescue by laughing. On the other hand, should the same pedestrian fall and fracture his skull the motor integration of the onlookers would be consumed by rendering physical assistance—hence there would be no laughter. In children almost any unexpected phenomenon, such as a sudden "booing" from behind a door, is attended by laughter, and in like manner the kinetic reaction produced by the innumerable threats of danger which are suddenly averted, a breach of the conventions, a sudden relief from acute nervous tension; a surprise—indeed, any excitant to which there is no predetermined method of giving a physical response— may be neutralized by the excitation of the mechanism of laughter.

In the same way the laughter excited by jokes may be explained. An analysis of a joke shows that it is composed of two parts—the first, in which is presented a subject that acts as a stimulus to action, and the second, in which the story turns suddenly so that the stimulus to action is unex-

pectedly withdrawn.   The subject matter of the joke affects
each hearer according to the type of stimuli that commonly
excites that individual.   Hence it is that a joke may convulse
one person while it bores another, and so there are jokes of

FIG. 32.—A STUDY IN EXPRESSION.
The camera excited resentment in one boy, which was expressed by crying;
amusement in the second; while the third was indifferent.

the classes, bankers' jokes, politicians' jokes, the jokes of
professional men, of the plebeian, of the artist, etc.   If the
joke fails, the integration products of the excitation may be
used in physical resentment (Fig. 32).

Another type of laughter is that associated with the

ticklish points of certain parts of the body, the soles of the feet and certain parts of the trunk and of the abdomen. The excitation of the ticklish receptors, like pain, compels self-defensive motor acts. This response is of phylogenetic origin, and may be awakened only by stimuli which are too light to be painful. In this connection it is of interest to note that a superficial, insect-like contact with the skin rarely provokes laughter, and that the tickling of the nasal, oral, and pulmonary tracts does not produce laughter. The ticklish points that cause laughter are rather deeply placed, and a certain type of physical contact is required to constitute an adequate stimulus. That is, the contact must arouse a phylogenetic association with a physical struggle or with physical exertion. In the foot, the adequate stimuli for laughter are such contacts as resemble or suggest piercing by stones or rough objects. The intention of the one who tickles must be known; if his intention be playful, laughter results, whereas if injury be intended, then an effort toward escape or defense is excited, but no laughter. If deep tickling of the ribs is known to be malicious, it will excite physical resentment and not laughter. Self-tickling rarely causes laughter for the reason that auto-tickling can cause only a known degree of stimulation, so that there results no excessive integration which requires relief by the neutral muscular activity of laughter. In fact, one never sees purposeful acts and laughter associated. According to its severity, an isolated stimulus causes either an action or laughter. The ticklish points in our bodies were probably developed as a means of defense against serious attacks and of escape from injurious contacts.

Anger, fear, and grief are also strong excitants and, therefore, are stimuli to motor activity. It is obvious that whatever the excitant the physico-chemical action of the brain and the ductless glands cannot be reversed—the effect of the stimulus cannot be recalled, therefore either a purposeful muscular act or a neutralizing act must be performed or else the liberated energy must smoulder in the various parts of the body.

It is on this hypothesis that the origin and the purpose of laughter and crying may be understood. Even a superficial analysis of the phenomena of both laughter and crying show them to be without any external motor purpose; the respiratory mechanism is intermittently stimulated and inhibited; and the shoulder and arm muscles, indeed, many muscles of the trunk and the extremities are, as far as any external design is concerned, purposelessly contracted and released until the kinetic energy mobilized by excitation is utilized. During this time the facial expression gives the index to the mental state.

Crying, like laughter, is always preceded by a stimulation to some motor action which may or may not be performed (Figs. 33 and 34). If a mother is anxiously watching the course of a serious illness of her child and if, in caring for it, she is stimulated to the utmost to perform motor acts, she will continue in a state of motor tenseness until the child recovers or dies. If relief is sudden, as in the crisis of pneumonia, and the mother is not exhausted, she will easily laugh; if tired, she may cry. If death occurs, the stimulus to motor acts is suddenly withdrawn and she then cries aloud, and performs many motor acts as a result of the intense stimulation to motor activity which is no longer needed in the physical care of her child. With this clue we can find the

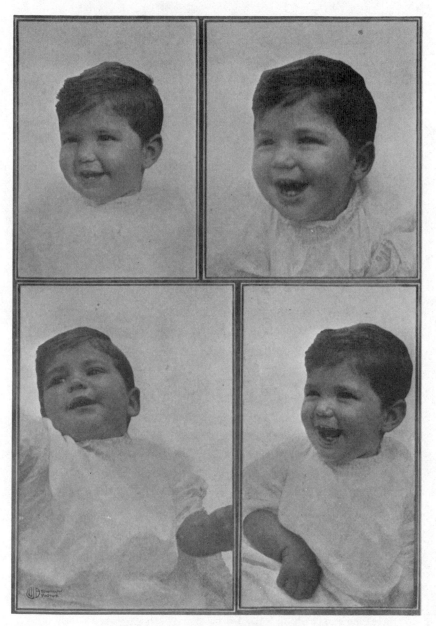

Fig. 33.—Laughing Child.

This baby is trying to seize the toy with which his sister is playing and finds relief in continuous activation.

103

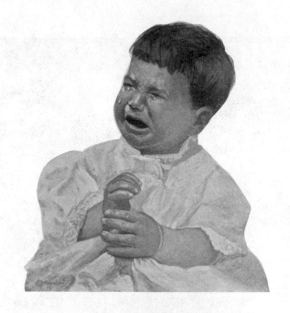

B

FIG. 34.—CRYING CHILD.

That crying is the result of stimulation to motor activity is well shown by these photographs. In A the baby's bottle is being held just beyond his reach, and the position of his hands shows that he is ready to take it, but as it is not given to him, his activation finds expression in moderate crying.

In B the bottle has been carried out of his sight, the activation has increased and is expressed by increased crying and by rapid arm motions.

explanation of many phenomena. We can understand why
laughter and crying are so frequently interchangeable; why
they often blend and why either gives a sense of relief; we

FIG. 35.—SLEEPING CHILD.
The energy expended in his waking activities is being restored in sleep. Compare with Figs. 33 and 34.

can understand why either laughter or crying can come only
when the issue that causes the integration is determined;
we can understand the extraordinary tendency to laughter
that discloses the unspoken sentiments of love; we can

understand the tears of the woman when she receives a proposal of marriage from the man she loves; we can understand why any averted circumstance, such as a threatened breach of the conventions, which would have led to embarrassment or humiliation, leads to a tendency to laughter; and why the recital of heroic deeds by association leads to tears. On the other hand, under the domination of acute diseases, of acute fear, or of great exhaustion, there is usually neither laughter nor crying because the nervous system is under the control of a dominating influence as a result of which the body is so exhausted that the excess of energy which alone can produce laughing or crying is lacking.

A remarkable study of the modification of laughter and crying by disease is found in that most interesting of diseases —exophthalmic goiter. In this disease there is a low threshold to all stimuli. That the very motor mechanism of which we have been speaking is involved, is shown by an enormous increase in its activity. There is also an increase in the size of certain at least of the activating glands—the thyroid and the adrenals are enlarged and overactive and the glycogen-producing function of the liver is stimulated. The most striking phenomenon of this disease, however, is the remarkable lowering of the brain thresholds to stimuli. In other words, in Graves' disease the nervous system and the activating glands—the entire motor mechanism—are in an exalted state of activity.

If this be true, then these patients should exhibit behavior precisely contrary to that of those suffering from acute infection, that is, they should be constantly clearing their systems of these superabundant energizing materials by crying or laughing, and this is precisely what happens—the flood-gates of tears are open much of the time in Graves' disease—a disease of the emotions.

We have already interpreted pain as a phenomenon of motor activity. When pain does not lead to muscular activity it therefore frequently leads to crying or to moaning, just as tickling, which is equally an incentive to motor activity, results in laughter if it does not find full expression in action.

From the foregoing we infer that pain, the intense motor response to tickling, and emotional excitation are all primitive biologic reactions for the good of the individual, and that all have their origin in the operation of the great laws of evolution. If to this inference we add the physiologic dictum that the nervous system always acts as a whole, and that it can respond to but one stimulus at a time, we can easily understand that while diverse causes may integrate the nervous system for a specific action, if the cause be suddenly removed, then the result of the integration of the nervous system may be, not a specific action, but an undesigned muscular action, such as crying or laughter. Hence it is that laughter and crying may be evoked by diverse exciting causes. The intensity of the laughter or of the crying depends upon the intensity of the stimulus and the dynamic state of the individual.

The linking together of these apparently widely separated phenomena by the simple law of the discharge of energy by association perhaps explains the association of an abnormal tendency to tears with an abnormally low threshold for pain (Fig. 36). In the neurasthenic, tears and pain are produced with abnormal facility. Hence it is that, if a patient about to undergo a surgical operation is in a state of fear and dread before the operation, the threshold to all stimuli is lowered, and this lowered threshold will continue throughout the operation, even under inhalation anesthesia, because the stimulus produced by cutting sensitive tissue is transmitted to the brain just as readily as if the patient were not anes-

FIG. 36.—Photo of homesick patient in hospital whose brain threshold had been so lowered that the slightest stimulus resulted in tears.

thetized. In like manner, the brain may be sensitized by the administration of large doses of thyroid extract prior to operation, the threshold to injury in such a case continuing to be low to traumatic stimuli even under anesthesia. Under the sensitizing influences of thyroid extract or of Graves' disease the effect of an injury, of an operation, or of emotional excitation is heightened. The extent to which the threshold to pain or to any other excitant is affected by Graves' disease is illustrated by the almost fatal reaction which I once saw result from the mere pricking with a hypodermic needle of a patient with this disease. As the result of a visit from a friend, the pulse-rate of a victim of this disease may increase twenty beats and his temperature rise markedly. I have seen the mere suggestion of an operation produce collapse. As the brain is thus remarkably sensitized in Graves' disease, we find that in these patients laughter, crying, emotional disturbances, and surgical shock are produced with remarkable facility.

I hope that even this admittedly crude and imperfect consideration of this subject will suggest the possibility of establishing a practical viewpoint as to the origin and purpose of pain, of tickling, and of such expressions of emotion as laughter and crying, and that it may help us to understand their significance in health and in disease.

THE RELATION BETWEEN THE PHYSICAL STATE OF THE BRAIN-CELLS AND BRAIN FUNCTIONS—EXPERIMENTAL AND CLINICAL *

The brain in all animals (including man) is but the clearing-house for reactions to environment, for animals are essentially motor or neuromotor mechanisms, composed of many parts, it is true, but integrated by the nervous system. Throughout the phylogenetic history of the race the stimuli of environment have driven this mechanism, whose seat of power—the battery—is the brain.

Since all normal life depends upon the response of the brain to the daily stimuli, we should expect in health, as well as in disease, to find modifications of the functions and the physical state of the component parts of this central battery—the brain-cells. Although we must believe, then, that every reaction to stimuli, however slight, produces a corresponding change in the brain-cells, yet there are certain normal, that is, non-diseased, conditions which produce especially striking changes. The cell changes due to the emotions, for example, are so similar, and in extreme conditions approach so closely to the changes produced by disease, that it is impossible to say where the normal ceases and the abnormal begins.

In view of the similarity of brain-cell changes it is not strange that in the clinic, as well as in daily life, we are confronted constantly by outward manifestations which are so nearly identical that the true underlying cause of the condi-

* Address before The American Philosophical Society, April 18, 1913.

tion in any individual case is too often overlooked or mis-
understood. In our laboratory experiments and in our
clinical observations we have found that exhaustion produced
by intense emotion, prolonged physical exertion, insomnia,
intense fear, certain toxemias, hemorrhage, and the condition commonly denominated surgical shock, produce
similar outward manifestations and identical brain-cell
changes.

It is, therefore, the purpose of this paper to present the
definite results of laboratory researches which show certain
relations between alterations in brain functions and physical
changes in the brain-cells.

Fear.—Our experiments have shown that the brain-cell
changes due to fear may be divided into two stages: First,
that of hyperchromatism—stimulation; second, that of
hypochromatism—exhaustion (Figs. 5 and 13). Hyperchromatism was shown only in the presence of the activating
stimuli or within a very short time after they had been received. This state gradually changed until the period of
maximum exhaustion was reached—about six hours later.
Then a process of reconstruction began and continued until
the normal state was again reached.

Fatigue.—Fatigue from overexertion produced in the
brain-cells like changes to those produced by fear, these
changes being proportional to the amount of exertion (Fig.
4). In the extreme stage of exhaustion from this cause we
found that the total quantity of Nissl substance was enormously reduced. When the exertion was too greatly prolonged, it took weeks or months for the cells to be restored
to their normal condition. We have proved, therefore, that
in exhaustion resulting from emotion or from physical work

a certain number of the brain-cells are permanently lost. This is the probable explanation of the fact that an athlete or a race-horse trained to the point of highest efficiency can reach his maximum record but once in his life. Under certain conditions, however, it is possible that, though some chromatin is forever lost, the remainder may be so remarkably developed that for a time at least it will compensate for that which is gone.

Hemorrhage.—The loss of blood from any cause, if sufficient to reduce the blood-pressure, will occasion a change in the brain-cells, provided that the period of hypotension lasts for more than five minutes. This time limit is a safeguard against permanent injury from the temporary hypotension which causes one to faint. If the hemorrhage be long continued and the blood-pressure be low, there will be a permanent loss of some of the brain-cells. This explains why an individual who has suffered from a prolonged hemorrhage will never again be restored to his original powers.

Drugs.—According to their effect upon the brain-cells, drugs may be divided into three classes: First, those that stimulate the brain-cells to increased activity, as strychnin (Fig. 37); second, those that chemically destroy the brain-cells, as alcohol and iodoform (Figs. 38 and 39); third, those that suspend the functions of the cells without damaging them, as nitrous oxid, ether, morphin. Our experiments have shown that the brain-cell changes induced by drugs of the first class are precisely the same as the cycle of changes produced by the emotions and by physical activity. We have found that strychnin, according to the dosage, causes convulsions ending in exhaustion and death; excitation followed by lassitude; stimulation without notable after-results; or

8

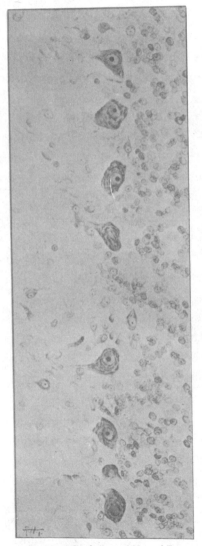

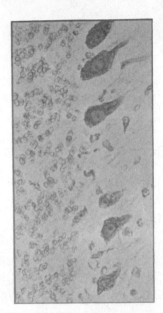

B, Section of Cerebellum of Dog after Single Dose of Strychnin.

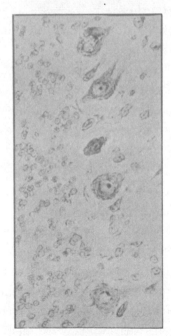

A, Section of Cerebellum of Normal Dog.

C, Section of Cerebellum of Dog after Repeated Doses of Strychnin.

Fig. 37.—Brain-cells Showing Stage of Hyperchromatism Followed by Chromatolysis Resulting from the Continuation of the Stimulus. (Camera lucida drawings.)

Fig. 38.

A

SECTION OF CEREBELLUM OF DOG—NORMAL (× 310).

B

SECTION OF CEREBELLUM OF DOG SHOWING THE EFFECT ON THE BRAIN-CELLS OF IODO-FORM POISONING (× 310).

Note the general hypochromatism and the diffusion of stain.

increased mental tone; while the brain-cells accurately display these physiologic alterations in proportional hyperchromatism in the active stages, and proportional chromatolysis in the stages of reaction. The biologic and therapeutic application of this fact is as obvious as it is important.

In our experiments, alcohol in large and repeated dosage caused marked morphologic changes in the brain-cells which went as far even as the destruction of some of the cells (Fig. 39). Ether, on the other hand, even after five hours of administration, produced no observable destructive changes in the brain-cells.

The effect of iodoform was peculiarly interesting, as it was the only drug that produced a rise of temperature. Its observed effect upon the brain-cells was that of wide-spread destruction.

Infections.—In every observation regarding the effect of pyogenic infections on dogs and on man we found that they caused definite and demonstrable lesions in certain cells of the nervous system, the most marked changes being in the cortex and the cerebellum (Fig. 40). For example, in fatal infections resulting from bowel obstruction, in peritonitis, and in osteomyelitis, the real lesion is in the brain-cells. We may, therefore, reasonably conclude that the lassitude, the diminished mental power, the excitability, irritability, restlessness, delirium, and unconsciousness which may be associated with acute infections, are due to physical changes in the brain-cells.

Graves' Disease.—In Graves' disease the brain-cells show marked changes which are apparently the same as those produced by overwork, by the emotions, and by strych-

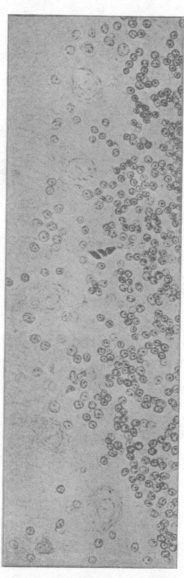

FIG. 39A.—SECTION OF HUMAN CEREBELLUM—NORMAL (AFTER ACCIDENTAL DEATH).

FIG. 39B.—SECTION OF HUMAN CEREBELLUM, SHOWING EFFECTS OF ALCOHOL (AFTER DEATH FROM DELIRIUM TREMENS). (Camera lucida drawings.)

Fig. 40.

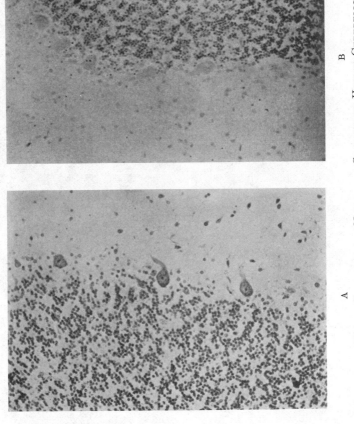

A

Section of Human Cerebellum—Normal (× 310).

B

Section of Human Cerebellum Showing the Effect on the Brain-cells of Acute Septicemia (× 310).

All are hypochromatic; nuclei and nucleoli have disappeared.

nin. In the postmortem examination of one advanced case it was found that a large number of brain-cells were disintegrated beyond the power of recuperation, even had the patient lived. This is undoubtedly the reason why a severe case of exophthalmic goiter sustains a permanent loss of brain power.

Insomnia.—The brains of rabbits which had been kept awake for one hundred hours showed precisely the same changes as those shown in physical fatigue, strychnin poisoning, and exhaustion from emotional stimulation. Eight hours of continuous sleep restored all the cells except those that had been completely exhausted. This will explain the permanent ill effect of long-continued insomnia; that is, long-continued insomnia permanently destroys a part of the brain-cells just as do too great physical exertion, certain drugs, emotional strain, exophthalmic goiter, and hemorrhage. We found, however, that if, instead of natural sleep, the rabbits were placed for the same number of hours under nitrous oxid anesthesia, not only did the brain-cells recover from the physical deterioration, but that 90 per cent. of them became hyperchromatic. This gives us a possible clue to the actual chemical effect of sleep. For since nitrous oxid owes its anesthetic effect to its influence upon oxidation, we may infer that sleep also retards the oxidation of the cell contents. If this be true, then it is probable that inhalation anesthetics exert their peculiar influence upon that portion of the brain through which sleep itself is produced. If nitrous oxid anesthesia and sleep are chemically identical, then we have a further clue to one of the primary mechanisms of life itself; and as a practical corollary one might be able to produce artificial sleep which would closely resemble normal sleep, but which would have this advantage, that by using an anesthetic which interferes with oxidation the brain-cells might be reconstructed after physical fatigue, after emotional strain, or after the depression of disease.

In the case of the rabbit in which nitrous oxid was substituted for sleep, the appearance of the brain-cells resembled that in but one other group experimentally examined—the brain-cells of hibernating woodchucks.

Insanity.—Our researches have shown that in the course of a fatal disease and in fatal exhaustion, however produced, death does not ensue until there is marked disorganization of the brain tissue. In the progress of disease or exhaustion one may see in different patients every outward manifestation of mental deterioration, manifestations which, in a person who does not show any other sign of physical disease, mark him as insane. Take, for example, the progressive mental state of a brilliant scholar suffering from typhoid fever. On the first day of the gradual onset of the disease he would notice that his mental power was below its maximum efficiency; on the second he would notice a further deterioration, and so the mental effect of his disease would progress until he would find it impossible to express a thought or to make a deduction. No one can be philanthropic with jaundice; no one suffering from Graves' disease can be generous; no mental process is possible in the course of the acute infectious diseases. Just prior to death from any cause every one is in a mental state which, if it could be continued, would cause that individual to be judged insane. If the delirium that occurs in the course of certain diseases should be continued, the patient would be judged insane. In severe cases of Graves' disease the patient is insane.

Individuals under overwhelming emotion may be temporarily insane. Every clinician has seen great numbers of cases in which insanity is a phase of a disease, of an injury, or of an emotion. The stage of excitation in anesthesia is insanity. The only difference between what is conventionally called insanity and the fleeting insanity of the sick and the injured is that of time. We may conclude, therefore, what must be the brain-picture of the person who is permanently insane. This *a priori* reasoning is all that is possible, since the study of the brain in the insane has thus far been confined to the brains of those who have died of some disease. And it is impossible to say which changes have been produced by the fatal disease, and which by the condition which produced the insanity. The only logical way by which to investigate the physical basis of insanity would be to make use of the very rare opportunities of studying the brains of insane persons who have died in accidents.

Our experiments have proved conclusively that whether we call a person fatigued or diseased, the brain-cells undergo physical deterioration, accompanied by loss of mental power (Figs. 40 to 43). Even to the minutest detail we can show a direct relationship between the physical state of the brain-cells and the mental power of the individual, that is, the physical power of a person goes *pari passu* with his mental power. Indeed, it is impossible to conceive how any mental action, however subtle, can occur without a corresponding change in the brain-cells. It is possible now to measure only the evidences of the effects on the brain-cells of gross and violent mental activity. At some future time it will doubtless be possible so to refine the technic of brain-cell examina-

Fig. 41.

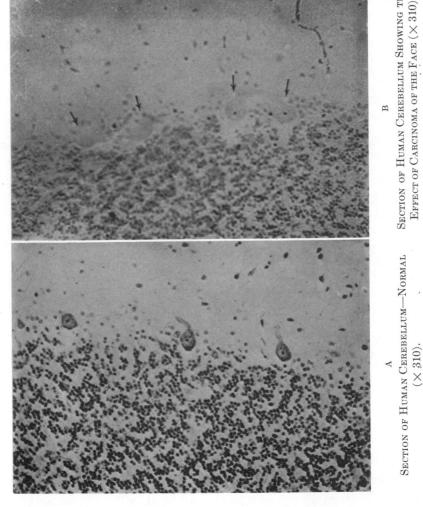

A

Section of Human Cerebellum—Normal (× 310).

B

Section of Human Cerebellum Showing the Effect of Carcinoma of the Face (× 310).

Note the lack of active cells. Some of the Pur-

Fig. 42.

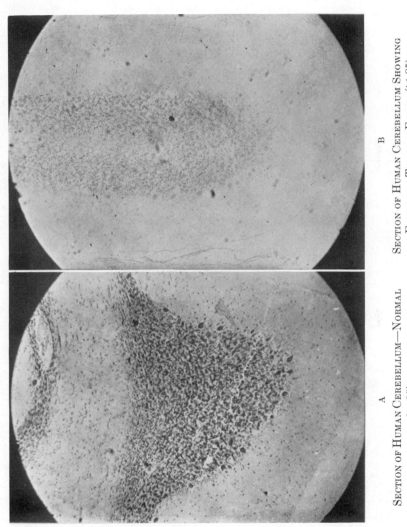

A

SECTION OF HUMAN CEREBELLUM—NORMAL
(× 85).

B

SECTION OF HUMAN CEREBELLUM SHOWING
EFFECT OF TYPHOID FEVER (× 85).

Note the almost complete disappearance of the Purkinje cells.

Fig. 43.

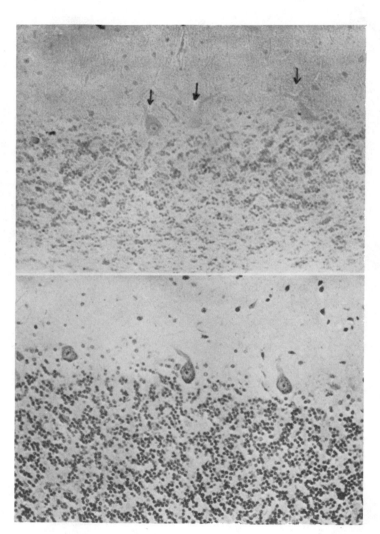

A

SECTION OF HUMAN CEREBELLUM—NORMAL
(× 310).

B

SECTION OF HUMAN CEREBELLUM SHOWING
THE EFFECT OF TYPHOID FEVER (× 310).

Compare the faint traces of the Purkinje cells which are indicated by arrows in B with the cells in

tions that more subtle changes may be measured. Nevertheless, with the means at our disposal we have shown already that in all the conditions which we have studied the cells of the cortex show the greatest changes, and that loss of the higher mental functions invariably accompanies the cell deterioration.

A MECHANISTIC VIEW OF PSYCHOLOGY *

Traditional religion, traditional medicine, and traditional psychology have insisted upon the existence in man of a triune nature. Three "ologies" have been developed for the study of each nature as a separate entity—body, soul, and spirit—physiology, psychology, theology; physician, psychologist, priest. To the great minds of each class, from the days of Aristotle and Hippocrates on, there have come glimmerings of the truth that the phenomena studied under these divisions were interrelated. Always, however, the conflict between votaries of these sciences has been sharp, and the boundary lines between them have been constantly changing. Since the great discoveries of Darwin, the zoölogist, biologist, and physiologist have joined hands, but still the soul-body-spirit chaos has remained. The physician has endeavored to fight the gross maladies which have been the result of disordered conduct; the psychologist has reasoned and experimented to find the laws governing conduct; and the priest has endeavored by appeals to an unknown god to reform conduct.

The great impulse to a deeper and keener study of man's relation, not only to man, but to the whole animal creation, which was given by Darwin, has opened the way to the study of man on a different basis. Psychologists, physicians, and priests are now joining hands as never before in the great

* Address delivered before Sigma Xi, Case School of Science, Cleveland, Ohio, May 27, 1913, and published in *Science*, August 29, 1913.

world-wide movement for the betterment of man. The new science of sociology is combining the functions of all three, for priest, physician, and psychologist have come to see that man is in large measure the product of his environment.

My thesis to-night, however, will go beyond this common agreement, for I shall maintain, not that man is in *large measure* the product of his environment, but that environment has been the actual *creator* of man; that the old division between body, soul, and spirit is non-existent; that man is a unified mechanism responding in every part to the adequate stimuli given it from without by the environment of the present and from within by the environment of the past, the record of which is stored in part in cells throughout the mechanism, but especially in its central battery—the brain. I postulate further that the human body mechanism is equipped, first, for such conflict with environment as will tend to the preservation of the individual; and, second, for the propagation of the species, both of these functions when most efficiently carried out tending to the upbuilding and perfection of the race.

Through the long ages of evolution the human mechanism has been slowly developed by the constant changes and growth of its parts which have resulted from its continual adaptation to its environment. In some animals the protection from too rough contact with surroundings was secured by the development of an outside armor; in others noxious secretions served the purposes of defense, but such devices as these were not suitable for the higher animals nor for the diverse and important functions of the human race. The safety of the higher animals and of man had to be preserved by some mechanism by means of which they could become adapted to a much wider and more complex environment, the dominance over which alone gives them their right to be called "superior beings." The mechanism by the progressive development of which living beings have been able to react more and more effectually to their environment is the central nervous system, which is seen in one of its simplest forms in motor plants, such as the sensitive plant and the Venus fly-trap, and in its highest development only in the sanest, healthiest, happiest, and most useful men.

The essential function of the nervous system was primarily to secure some form of motor activity, first as a means of securing food, and later as a means of escaping from enemies and to promote procreation. Activities for the preservation of the individual and of the species were and are the only purposes for which the body energy is expended. The central nervous system has accordingly been developed for the purpose of securing such motor activities as will best adapt the individuals of a species for their self-preservative conflict with environment.

It is easy to appreciate that the simplest expressions of nerve response—the reflexes—are motor in character, but it is difficult to understand how such intangible reactions as love, hate, poetic fancy, or moral inhibition can be also the result of the adaptation to environment of a distinctively motor mechanism. We expect, however, to prove that so-called "psychic" states as well as the reflexes are products of adaptation; that they occur automatically in response to adequate stimuli in the environment; that, like the reflexes, they are expressions of motor activity, which, although intangible and unseen, in turn incite to activity the units of the motor mechanism of the body; and finally, that any

9

"psychic" condition results in a definite depletion of the potential energy in the brain-cells which is proportionate to the muscular exertion of which it is the representative.

That this nerve mechanism may effectively carry out its twofold function, first, of self-adaptation to meet adequately the increasingly complicated stimuli of environment; and second, of adapting the motor mechanism to respond adequately to its demands, there have been implanted in the body numerous nerve ceptors—some for the transmission of stimuli harmful to the mechanism—nociceptors; some of a beneficial character—beneceptors; and still others more highly specialized, which partake of the nature of both bene- and nociceptors—the distance ceptors, or special senses.

A convincing proof that environment has been the creator of man is seen in the absolute adaptation of the nociceptors as manifested in their specific response to adequate stimuli, and in their presence in only those parts of the body which throughout the history of the race have been most exposed to harmful contacts. We find they are most numerous in the face, the neck, the abdomen, the hands, and the feet; while in the back they are few in number, and within the bony cavities they are lacking.

Instances of the specific responses made by the nociceptors might be multiplied indefinitely. Sneezing, for example, is a specific response made by the motor mechanism to stimulation of nociceptors in the nose, while stimulation of the larynx does not produce a sneeze, but a cough; stimulation of the nociceptors of the stomach does not produce cough, but vomiting; stimulation of the nociceptors of the intestine does not produce vomiting, but increased peristaltic action. There are no nociceptors misplaced; none wasted;

none that do not make an adequate response to adequate stimulation.

Another most significant proof that the environment of the past has been the creator of the man of to-day is seen in the fact that man has added to his environment certain factors to which adaptation has not as yet been made. For example, heat is a stimulus which has existed since the days of prehistoric man, while the x-ray is a discovery of to-day; to heat, the nociceptors produce an adequate response; to the x-ray there is no response. There was no weapon in the prehistoric ages which could move at the speed of a bullet from the modern rifle, therefore, while slow penetration of the tissues produces great pain and muscular response, there is no response to the swiftly moving bullet.

The response to contact stimuli then depends always on the presence of nociceptors in the affected part of the body and to the type of the contact. Powerful response is made to crushing injury by environmental forces; to such injuring contacts as resemble the impacts of fighting; to such tearing injuries as resemble those made by teeth and claws (Fig. 9). On the other hand, the sharp division of tissue by cutting produces no adaptive response; indeed, one might imagine that the body could be cut to pieces by a superlatively sharp knife applied at tremendous speed without material adaptive response.

These examples indicate how the history of the phylogenetic experiences of the human race may be learned by a study of the position and the action of the nociceptors, just as truly as the study of the arrangement and variations in the strata of the earth's crust discloses to us geologic history.

These adaptive responses to stimuli are the result of the

action of the brain-cells, which are thus continually played upon by the stimuli of environment. The energy stored in the brain-cells in turn activates the various organs and parts of the body. If the environmental impacts are repeated with such frequency that the brain-cells have no time for restoration between them, the energy of the cells becomes exhausted and a condition of shock results. Every action of the body may thus be analyzed into a stimulation of ceptors, a consequent discharge of brain-cell energy, and a final adaptive activation of the appropriate part. Walking, running, and their modifications constitute an adaptation of wonderful perfection, for, as Sherrington has shown, the adaptation of locomotion consists of a series of reflexes— ceptors in the joints, in the limb, and in the foot being stimulated by variations in pressure.

As we have shown, the bene- and nociceptors orientate man to all forms of physical contact—the former *guide him to* the acquisition of food and to sexual contact; the latter *direct him from* contacts of a harmful nature. The distance ceptors, on the other hand, adapt man to his distant environment by means of communication through unseen forces— ethereal vibrations produce sight; air waves produce sound; microscopic particles of matter produce smell. The advantage of the distance ceptors is that they allow time for orientation, and because of this great advantage the majority of man's actions are responses to their adequate stimuli. As Sherrington has stated, the greater part of the brain has been developed by means of stimuli received through the special senses, especially through the light ceptors, the optic nerves.

We have just stated that by means of the distance ceptors

animals and man orientate themselves to their distant environment. As a result of the stimulation of the special senses chase and escape are effected, fight is conducted, food is secured, and mates are found. It is obvious, therefore, that the distance ceptors are the primary cause of continuous and exhausting expenditures of energy. On the other hand, stimuli applied to contact ceptors lead to short, quick discharges of nervous energy. The child puts his hand in the fire and there is an immediate and complete response to the injuring contact; he sees a pot of jam on the pantry shelf and a long train of continued activities are set in motion, leading to the acquisition of the desired object.

The contact ceptors do not at all promote the expenditure of energy in the chase or in fight, in the search for food or for mates. Since the distance ceptors control these activities, one would expect to find that they control also those organs whose function is the production of energizing internal secretions. Over these organs—the thyroid, the adrenals, the hypophysis—the contact ceptors have no control. Prolonged laboratory experimentation seems to prove this postulate. According to our observations, no amount of physical trauma inflicted upon animals will cause hyperthyroidism or increased adrenalin in the blood, while fear and rage do produce hyperthyroidism and increased adrenalin (Fig. 44) (Cannon). This is a statement of far-reaching importance and is the key to an explanation of many chronic diseases—diseases which are associated with the intense stimulation of the distance ceptors in human relations.

Stimuli of the contact ceptors differ from stimuli of the distance ceptors in still another important particular. The

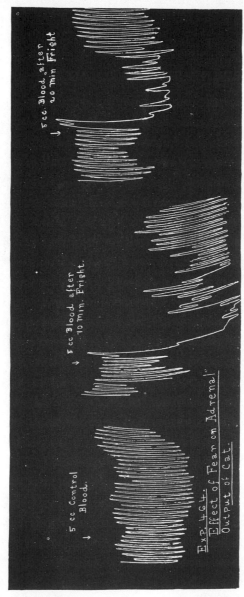

Control blood negative; no adrenalin present.

Positive adrenalin reaction produced by fright of ten minutes' duration.

Adrenalin still present, but in lesser amounts under the influence of the longer period of fright. The glands had probably become partly exhausted.

FIG. 44.—CANNON TEST FOR ADRENALIN, SHOWING REACTION OF THE ADRENAL GLANDS TO STIMULATION—FEAR.

adequacy of stimuli of the contact ceptors depends upon their number and intensity, while the adequacy of the stimuli of the distance ceptors depends upon the *experience* of the species and of the individual. That is, according to phylogeny and ontogeny this or that sound, this or that smell, this or that sight, through association recapitulates the experience of the species and of the individual—awakens the phylogenetic and ontogenetic memory. In other words, sights, sounds, and odors are symbols which awaken phylogenetic association. If a species has become adapted to make a specific response to a certain object, then that response will occur automatically in an individual of that species when he hears, sees, or smells that object. Suppose, for example, that the shadow of a hawk were to fall simultaneously on the eyes of a bird, a rabbit, a cow, and a boy. That shadow would at once activate the rabbit and the bird to an endeavor to escape, each in a specific manner according to its phylogenetic adaptation; the cow would be indifferent and neutral; while the boy, according to his personal experience or ontogeny, might remain neutral, might watch the flight of the hawk with interest or might try to shoot it.

Each phylogenetic and each ontogenetic experience by an indirect method develops its own mechanism of adaptation in the brain; and the brain threshold is raised or lowered to stimuli by the strength and frequency of repetition of the experience. Thus through the innumerable symbols supplied by environment the distance ceptors drive this or that animal according to the type of brain pattern and the particular state of threshold which has been developed in that animal by its phylogenetic and ontogenetic experiences. The brain pattern depends upon his phylogeny, the state of threshold upon his ontogeny. Each *brain pattern* is created by some particular element in the environment to which an adaptation has been made for the good of the species. The *state of threshold* depends upon the effect made upon the individual by his personal contacts with that particular element in his environment. The presence of that element produces in the individual an associative recall of the adaptation of his species—that is, the brain pattern developed by his phylogeny becomes energized to make a specific response. The intensity of the response depends upon the state of threshold —that is, upon the associative recall of the individual's own experience—his ontogeny.

If the full history of the species and of the individual could be known in every detail, then every detail of that individual's conduct in health and disease could be predicted. Reaction to environment is the basis of conduct, of moral standards, of manners and conventions, of work and play, of love and hate, of protection and murder, of governing and being governed, in fact, of all the reactions between human beings—of the entire web of life. To quote Sherrington once more: "Environment drives the brain, the brain drives the various organs of the body."

By what means are these adaptations made? What is the mechanism through which adequate responses are made to the stimuli received by the ceptors? We postulate that in the brain there are innumerable patterns each the mechanism for the performance of a single kind of action, and that the brain-cells supply the energy—electric or otherwise—by which the act is performed; that the energy stored in the brain-cells is in some unknown manner released by the force which activates the brain pattern; and that through an unknown property of these brain patterns each stimulus causes such a change that the next stimulus of the same kind passes with greater facility.

Each separate motor action presumably has its own mechanism—brain pattern—which is activated by but one ceptor and by that ceptor only when physical force of a certain intensity and rate of motion is applied. This is true both of the visible contacts affecting the nociceptors and of the invisible contacts by those intangible forces which affect the distance ceptors. For example, each variation in speed of the light-producing waves of ether causes a specific reaction in the brain. For one speed of ether waves the reaction is the perception of the color blue; for another, yellow; for another, violet. Changes in the speed of air waves meet with specific response in the brain patterns tuned to receive impressions through the aural nerves, and so we distinguish differences in sound pitch. If we can realize the infinite delicacy of the mechanisms adapted to these infinitesimal variations in the speed and intensity of invisible and intangible stimuli, it will not be difficult to conceive the variations of brain patterns which render possible the specific responses to the coarser contacts of visible environment.

Each brain pattern is adapted for but one type of motion, and so the specific stimuli of the innumerable ceptors play each upon its own brain pattern only. In addition, each brain pattern can react to stimuli applied only within certain limits. Too bright a light blinds; too loud a sound deafens. No mechanism is adapted for waves of light above or below a certain rate of speed, although this range varies in different individuals and in different species according to the training of the individual and the need of the species.

We have already referred to the fact that there is no receptive mechanism adapted to the stimuli from the x-ray, from the high-speed bullet, from electricity. So, too, there are innumerable forces in nature which can excite in man no adaptive response, since there exist in man no brain patterns tuned to their waves, as in the case of certain ethereal and radioactive forces.

On this mechanistic basis the emotions may be explained as activations of the entire motor mechanism for fighting, for escaping, for copulating. The sight of an enemy stimulates in the brain those patterns formed by the previous experiences of the individual with that enemy, and also the experiences of the race whenever an enemy had to be met and overcome. Each of these many brain patterns in turn activates that part of the body through which lies the path of its own adaptive response—those parts including the special energizing or activating organs. Laboratory experiments show that in an animal driven strongly by emotion the following changes may be seen: (1) A mobilization of the energy-giving compound in the brain-cells, evidenced by a primary increase of the Nissl substance and a later disappearance of this substance and the deterioration of the cells (Figs. 5 and 13); (2) increased output of adrenalin (Cannon), of thyroid secretion, of glycogen, and an increase of the power of oxidation in the muscles; (3) accelerated circulation and respiration with increased body temperature; (4) altered metabolism. All these are adaptations to increase the motor efficiency of the mechanism. In addition, we find an inhibition of the functions of every organ and tissue that consumes energy, but does not contribute directly to motor efficiency. The mouth becomes dry; the gastric and pancreatic secretions are lessened or are completely inhibited; peristaltic action stops. The obvious purpose of all these activations and inhibitions is to mass every atom of energy upon the muscles that are conducting the defense or attack.

So strong is the influence of phylogenetic experience that though an enemy to-day may not be met by actual physical attack, yet the decks are cleared for action, as it were, and the weapons made ready, the body as a result being shaken and exhausted. The type of emotion is plainly declared by the activation of the muscles which would be used if the appropriate physical action were consummated. In anger the teeth are set, the fists are clenched, the posture is rigid; in fear the muscles collapse, the joints tremble, and the running mechanism is activated for flight; in sexual excitement the mimicry is as obvious. The emotions, then, are the preparations for phylogenetic activities. If the activities are consummated, the fuel—glycogen—and the activating secretions from the thyroid, the adrenals, the hypophysis are consumed. In the activation without action, these products must be eliminated as waste products and so a heavy strain is put upon the organs of elimination. It is obvious that the body under emotion might be clarified by active muscular exercise, but the subject of the emotion is so strongly integrated thereby that it is difficult for him to engage in diverting, clarifying exertion. The person in anger does not want to be saved from the ill effects of his own emotion; he wants only to fight; the person in fear wants only to escape; the person under sexual excitement wants only possession.

All the lesser emotions—worry, jealousy, envy, grief, disappointment, expectation—all these influence the body in this manner, the consequences depending upon the intensity of the emotion and its protraction. Chronic emotional stimulation, therefore, may fatigue or exhaust the brain and may cause cardiovascular disease, indigestion, Graves' disease, diabetes, and insanity even.

The effect of the emotions upon the body mechanism may be compared to that produced upon the mechanism of an automobile if its engines are kept running at full speed while the machine is stationary. The whole machine will be shaken and weakened, the batteries and weakest parts being the first to become impaired and destroyed, the length of usefulness of the automobile being correspondingly limited.

We have shown that the effects upon the body mechanism of the action of the various ceptors is in relation to the response made by the *brain* to the stimuli received. What is this power of response on the part of the brain but *consciousness?* If this is so, then consciousness itself is a reaction to environment, and its intensity must vary with the state of the brain and with the environmental stimuli. If the brain-cells are in the state of highest efficiency, if their energy has not been drawn upon, then consciousness is at its height; if the brain is fatigued, that is, if the energy stored in the cells has been exhausted to any degree, then the intensity of consciousness is diminished. So degrees of consciousness vary from the height maintained by cells in full vigor through the stages of fatigue to sleep, to the deeper unconsciousness secured by the administration of inhalation anesthetics, to that complete unconsciousness of the environment which is secured by blocking the advent to the brain of all impressions from both distance and contact ceptors, by the use of both local and inhalation anesthetics —the state of anoci-association (Fig. 14).

Animals and man may be so exhausted as to be only semiconscious. While a brain perfectly refreshed by a long sleep cannot immediately sleep again, the exhausted brain and the refreshed brain when subjected to equal stimuli will rise to unequal heights of consciousness. The nature of the physical basis of consciousness has been sought in experiments on rabbits which were kept awake from one hundred to one hundred and nine hours. At the end of this time they were in a state of extreme exhaustion and seemed semiconscious. If the wakefulness had been further prolonged, this state of semi-consciousness would have steadily changed until it culminated in the permanent unconsciousness of death. An examination of the brain-cells of these animals showed physical changes identical with those produced by exhaustion from other causes, such as prolonged physical exertion or emotional strain (Figs. 45 and 46). After one hundred hours of wakefulness the rabbits were allowed a long period of sleep. All the brain-cells were restored except those that had been in a state of complete exhaustion. A single séance of sleep served to restore some of the cells, but those which had undergone extreme changes required prolonged rest. These experiments give us a definite physical basis for explaining the cost to the body mechanism of maintaining the conscious state. We have stated that the brain-cell changes produced by prolonged consciousness are identical with those produced by physical exertion and by emotional strain. Rest, then, and especially sleep, is needed to restore the physical state of the bra n-cells which have been impaired, and as the brain-cells constitute the central

Fig. 45.

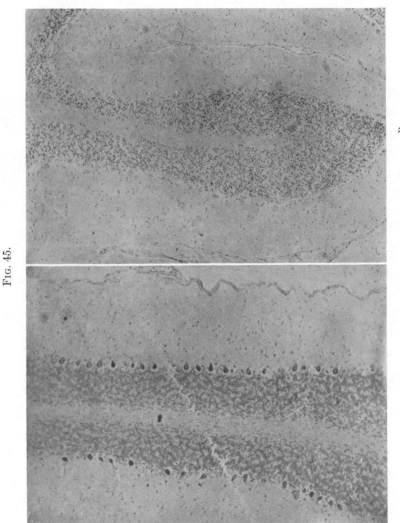

A

Section of Normal Cerebellum of Rabbit (× 100).

B

Section of Cerebellum of Rabbit after Insomnia—One Hundred and Nine Hours (× 100).

Compare the well-stained, clearly defined Purkinje cells in A with the faint traces of the Purkinje cells

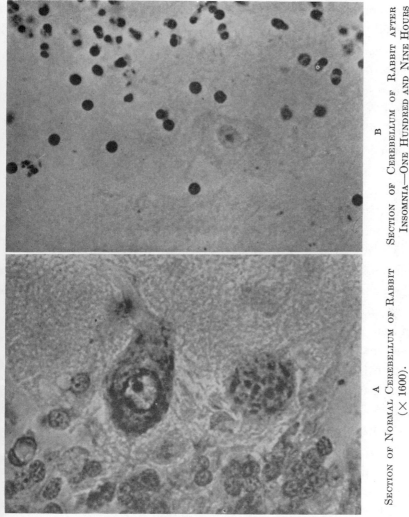

A

SECTION OF NORMAL CEREBELLUM OF RABBIT (× 1600).

B

SECTION OF CEREBELLUM OF RABBIT AFTER INSOMNIA—ONE HUNDRED AND NINE HOURS (× 1600).

Note the disappearance of the cell membrane and the faint nucleus and nucleolus in B in the only Purkinje cell in focus.

battery of the body mechanism, their restoration is essential for the maintenance of normal vitality.

In ordinary parlance, by consciousness we mean the activity of that part of the brain in which associative memory resides, but while associative memory is suspended the activities of the brain as a whole are by no means suspended; the respiratory and circulatory centers are active, as are those centers which maintain muscular tone. This is shown by the muscular response to external stimuli made by the normal person in sleep; by the occasional activation of motor patterns which may break through into consciousness causing dreams; and finally by the responses of the motor mechanism made to the injuring stimuli of an operation on a patient under inhalation anesthesia only.

Direct proof of the mechanistic action of many of life's phenomena is lacking, but the proof is definite and final of the part that the brain-cells play in maintain ng consciousness; of the fact that the degree of consciousness and mental efficiency depends upon the physical state of the brain-cells; and finally that efficiency may be restored by sleep, provided that exhaustion of the cells has not progressed too far. In this greatest phenomenon of life, then, the mechanistic theory is in harmony with the facts.

Perhaps no more convincing proof of our thesis that the body is a mechanism developed and adapted to its purposes by environment can be secured than by a study of that most constant manifestation of consciousness—pain.

Like the other phenomena of life, pain was undoubtedly evolved for a particular purpose—surely for the good of the individual. Like fear and worry, it frequently is injurious. What then may be its purpose?

We postulate that pain is a result of contact ceptor stimulation for the purpose of securing protective muscular activity. This postulate applies to all kinds of pain, whatever their cause—whether physical injury, pyogenic infection, the obstruction of hollow viscera, childbirth, etc.

All forms of pain are associated with muscular action, and as in every other stimulation of the ceptors, each kind of pain is specific to the causative stimuli. The child puts his hand in the fire; physical injury pain results, and the appropriate muscular response is elicited. If pressure is prolonged on some parts of the body, anemia of the parts may result, with a corresponding discomfort or pain, requiring muscular action for relief. When the rays of the sun strike directly upon the retina, light pain causes an immediate protective action; so too in the evacuation of the intestine and the urinary bladder as normal acts, and in overcoming obstruction of these tracts, discomfort or pain compel the required muscular actions. This view of pain as a stimulation to motor action explains why only certain types of infection are associated with pain; namely, those types in which the infection may be spread by muscular action or those in which the fixation of parts by continued muscular rigidity is an advantage. As a further remarkable proof of the marvelous adaptation of the body mechanism to meet varying environmental conditions, we find that just as nociceptors have been implanted in only those parts of the body which have been subject to nocuous contacts, so a type of infection which causes muscular action in one part of the body may cause none when it attacks another.

This postulate gives us the key to the pain-muscular phenomena of peritonitis, pleurisy, cystitis, cholecystitis,

10

etc., as well as to the pain-muscular phenomena in obstructions of the hollow viscera.   If pain is a part of a muscular response and occurs only as a result of contact ceptor stimulation by physical injury, infection, anemia, or obstruction, we may well inquire which part of the nerve mechanism is the site of the phenomenon of pain.   Is it the nerve-ending, the nerve-trunk, or the brain?   That is, is pain associated with the physical contact with the nerve-ending, or with the physical act of transmission along the nerve-trunk, or with the change of brain-cell substance by means of which the. motor-producing energy is released?

We postulate that the pain is associated with the discharge of energy from the brain-cells.   If this be true, then if every nociceptor in the body were equally stimulated in such a manner that all the stimuli should reach the brain-cells simultaneously, then the cells would find themselves in equilibrium and no motor act would be performed.   But if all the pain nerve ceptors but one were equally stimulated, and this one more strongly stimulated than the rest, then this one would gain possession of the final common path— would cause a muscular action and the sensation of pain.

It is well known that when a greater pain or stimulus is thrown into competition with a lesser one, the lesser is submerged.   Of this fact the school-boy makes use when he initiates the novice into the mystery of the painless pulling of hair.   The simultaneous but severe application of the boot to the blindfolded victim takes complete but exclusive possession of the final common path and the hair is painlessly plucked as a result of the triumph of the boot stimulus over the pull on the hair in the struggle for the final common path.

Persons who have survived a sudden, complete exposure to superheated steam, or whose bodies have been enwrapped in flame, testify that they have felt no pain. As this absence of pain may be due to the fact that the emotion of fear gained the final common path, to the exclusion of all other stimuli, we are trying by experimentation to discover the effects of simultáneous painful stimulation of all parts of the body. The data already in hand, and the experiments now in progress, in which anesthetized animals are subjected to powerful stimuli applied to certain parts of the body only, or simultaneously to all parts of the body, lead us to believe that in the former case the brain-cells become stimulated or hyperchromatic, while in the latter case no brain-cell changes occur. We believe that our experiments will prove that an equal and simultaneous stimulation of all parts of the body leaves the brain-cells in a state of equilibrium. Our theory of pain will then be well sustained, not only by common observation, but by experimental proof, and so the mechanistic view will be found in complete harmony with another important reaction.

We have stated that when a number of contact stimuli act simultaneously, the strongest stimulus will gain possession of the final common path—the path of action. When, however, stimuli of the distance ceptors compete with stimuli of the contact ceptors, the contact-ceptor stimuli often secure the common path, not because they are stronger or more important, but because they are immediate and urgent. In many instances, however, the distance-ceptor stimuli are strong, have the advantage of a lowered threshold, and therefore compete successfully with the immediate and present stimuli of the contact ceptors. In such cases we have the interesting phenomenon of physical injury without resultant pain or muscular response. The distance-ceptor stimuli which may thus triumph over even powerful contact-ceptor stimuli are those causing strong emotions—as great anger in fighting; great fear in a battle; intense sexual excitement. Dr. Livingstone has testified to his complete unconsciousness to pain during his struggle with a lion; although he was torn by teeth and claws, his fear overcame all other impressions. By frequently repeated stimulation the Dervish secures a low threshold to the emotions caused by the thought of God or the devil, and his emotional excitement is increased by the presence of others under the same stimulation; emotion, therefore, secures the final common path and he is unconscious of pain when he lashes, cuts, and bruises his body. The phenomena of hysteria may be explained on this basis, as may the unconsciousness of passing events in a person in the midst of a great and overwhelming grief. By constant practice the student may secure the final common path for such impressions as are derived from the stimuli offered by the subject of his study, and so he will be oblivious of his surroundings. Concentration is but another name for a final common path secured by the repetition and summation of certain stimuli.

If our premises are sustained, then we can recognize in man no will, no ego, no possibility for spontaneous action, for every action must be a response to the stimuli of contact or distance ceptors, or to their recall through associative memory. Memory is awakened by symbols which represent any of the objects or forces associated with the act recalled. Spoken and written words, pictures, sounds, may stimulate the brain patterns formed by previous stimulation of the distance ceptors; while touch, pain, temperature, pressure, may recall previous contact-ceptor stimuli. Memory depends in part upon the adequacy of the symbol, and in part upon the state of the threshold. If one has ever been attacked by a snake, the threshold to any symbol which could recall that attack would be low; the later recall of anything associated with the bite or its results would produce in memory a recapitulation of the whole scene, while even harmless snakes would thereafter be greeted with a shudder. On the other hand, in a child the threshold is low to the desire for the possession of any new and strange object; in a child, therefore, to whom a snake is merely an unusual and fascinating object, there is aroused only curiosity and the desire for the possession of a new plaything.

If we are to attribute to man the possession of a governing attribute not possessed by other parts of the animal creation, where are we to draw the boundary line, and say "here the ego—the will—the reason—emerges"? What attribute, after all, has man which in its ultimate analysis is not possessed by the lowest animals or by the vegetable creation, even? From the ameba, on through all the stages of animal existence, every action is but a response to an adequate stimulus; and as a result of adequate stimuli each step has been taken toward the higher and more intricate mechanisms which play the higher and more intricate parts in the great scheme of nature.

The Venus fly-trap responds to as delicate a stimulus as do any of the contact ceptors of animals, and the motor activity resulting from the stimulus is as complex. To an insect-like touch the plant responds; to a rough contact there is no response; that is, the motor mechanism of the plant has become attuned to only such stimuli as simulate the contact of those insects which form its diet. It catches flies, eats and digests them, and ejects the refuse (Fig. 47). The ameba does no less. The frog does no more, excepting that in its place in creation a few more reactions are required for its sustenance and for the propagation of its species. Man does no more, excepting that in man's manifold relations there are innumerable stimuli, for meeting which adequately, innumerable mechanisms have been evolved. The motor mechanism of the fly-trap is perfectly adapted to its purpose. The motor mechanism of man is adapted to its manifold uses, and as new environmental influences surround him, we must believe that new adaptations of the mechanism will be evolved to meet the new conditions.

Is not this conception of man's activities infinitely more wonderful, and infinitely more comprehensible than is the conception that his activities may be accounted for by the existence of an unknown, unimaginable, and intangible force called "mind" or "soul"?

We have already shown how the nerve mechanism is so well adapted to the innumerable stimuli of environment that it can accurately transmit and distinguish between the infinite variations of speed in the ether waves producing light, and the air waves producing sound. Each rate of vibration energizes only the mechanism which has been attuned to it. With marvelous accuracy the light and sound waves gain access to the nerve tissue and are finally interpreted in terms of motor responses, each by the brain pattern attuned to that particular speed and intensity. So stimuli and resultant actions multiplied by the total number of the

FIG. 47.—VENUS' FLY-TRAP—*Diancæa muscipula* (Linnæus).

When an insect alights upon a leaf, the leaf closes upon it like a spring trap in a few seconds and digests the insect, taking, perhaps, a fortnight over a meal.   Detail—lateral view of expanded leaf.

motor patterns in the brain of man give us the sum total of his life's activities—they constitute his life.

As in evolutionary history the permanence of an adaptation of the body mechanism depends upon its value in the preservation of the life of the individual and upon its power to increase the value of the individual to the race, so the importance and truth of these postulates and theories may well be judged on the same basis.

The fundamental instincts of all living matter are self-preservation and the propagation of the species. The instinct for self-preservation causes a plant to turn away from cold and damaging winds toward the life-giving sun; the inert mussel to withdraw within its shell; the insect to take flight; the animal to fight or to flee; and man to procure food that he may oppose starvation, to shelter himself and to provide clothes that he may avoid the dangers of excessive cold and heat, to combat death from disease by seeking medical aid, to avoid destruction by man or brute by fight or by flight. The instinct to propagate the species leads brute man by crude methods, and cultured man by methods more refined, to put out of his way sex rivals so that his own life may be continued through offspring. The life of the species is further assured by the protective action exercised over the young by the adults of the species. As soon as the youngest offspring is able successfully to carry on his own struggle with environment there is no longer need for the parent, and the parent enters therefore the stage of disintegration. The average length of life in any species is the sum of the years of immaturity, plus the years of female fertility, plus the adolescent years of the offspring.

The stimuli resulting from these two dominant instincts

are now so overpowering as compared with all other environmental stimuli that the mere possession of adequate knowledge of the damaging effects of certain actions as compared with the saving effects of others will (other things being equal) lead the individual to choose the right,—the self- and species-preservative course of action, instead of the wrong,—the self- and species-destructive course of action.

The dissemination of the knowledge of the far-reaching deleterious effects of protracted emotional strain, of overwork, and of worry will automatically raise man's threshold to the damaging activating stimuli causing the strong emotions, and will cause him to avoid dangerous strains of every kind.   The individual thus protected will therefore rise to a plane of poise and efficiency far above that of his uncontrolled fellows, and by so much will his efficiency, health, and happiness be augmented.

A full acceptance of this theory cannot fail to produce in those in whose charge rests the welfare of the young, an overwhelming desire to surround children with those environmental stimuli only which will tend to their highest ultimate welfare.

Such is the stimulating force of tradition that many who have been educated under the tenets of traditional beliefs will oppose these hypotheses—even violently, it may be. So they have opposed them; so they opposed Darwin; so they have opposed all new and apparently revolutionary doctrines.   Yet these persons themselves are by their very actions proving the efficiency of the vital principles which we have enunciated.   What is the whole social welfare movement but a recognition on the part of municipalities, educational boards, and religious organizations of the fact that the future welfare of the race depends upon the administration to the young of forceful uplifting environmental stimuli?

There are now, as there were in Darwin's day, many who feel that man is degraded from his high estate by the conception that he is not a reasoning, willing being, the result of a special creation. But one may wonder indeed what conception of the origin of man can be more wonderful or more inspiring than the belief that he has been slowly evolved through the ages, and that all creatures have had a part in his development; that each form of life has contributed and is contributing still to his present welfare and to his future advancement.

Recapitulation

Psychology,—the science of the human soul and its relations,—under the mechanistic theory of life, must receive a new definition. It becomes a science of man's activities as determined by the environmental stimuli of his phylogeny and of his ontogeny.

On this basis we postulate that throughout the history of the race nothing has been lost, but that every experience of the race and of the individual has been retained for the guidance of the individual and of the race; that for the accomplishment of this end there has been evolved through the ages a nerve mechanism of such infinite delicacy and precision that in some unknown manner it can register permanently within itself every impression received in the phylogenetic and ontogenetic experience of the individual; that each of these nerve mechanisms or brain patterns has its own connection with the external world, and that each is attuned to receive impressions of but one kind, as in the apparatus of wireless telegraphy each instrument can receive and interpret waves of a certain rate of intensity only; that thought, will, ego, personality, perception, imagination, reason, emotion, choice, memory, are to be interpreted in terms of these brain patterns; that these so-called phenomena of human life depend upon the stimuli which can secure the final common path, this in turn having been determined by the frequency and the strength of the environmental stimuli of the past and of the present.

Finally, as for life's origin and life's ultimate end, we are content to say that they are unknown, perhaps unknowable. We know only that living matter, like lifeless matter, has its own place in the cosmic processes; that the gigantic forces which operated to produce a world upon which life could exist, as a logical sequence, when the time was ripe, evolved life; and finally that these cosmic forces are still active, though none can tell what worlds and what races may be the result of their coming activities.

A MECHANISTIC THEORY OF DISEASE*

The human body is an elaborate mechanism equipped first for such conflict with environment as will tend to the preservation of the individual, and second for the propagation of the species, both of these functions, when most efficiently carried out, tending to the upbuilding and perfection of the race. From the date of Harvey's discovery of the circulation of the blood, to the present day, the human body has been constantly compared to a machine, but the time for analogy and comparison is past. I postulate that the body *is* itself a mechanism responding in every part to the adequate stimuli given it from without by the environment of the present and from within by the environment of the past, the memory of which is stored in the central battery of the mechanism—the brain.

* * * * * * * * * * *

* * * * * * * * * * *

If the full history of the species and of the individual could be known in every detail, then every detail of that individual's conduct in health and disease could be predicted. Reaction to environment is the basis of conduct, of moral standards, of manners and conventions, of work and play, of love and hate,

* Oration in Surgery. Delivered at the 147th Annual Meeting of the Medical Society of New Jersey, at Spring Lake, N. J., June 11, 1913.
  In this address the paragraphs which were taken from the preceding paper, "A Mechanistic View of Psychology," have been omitted, those portions only being republished in which the premises have been applied in a discussion of certain medical problems rather than of psychological problems.

of protection and murder, of governing and being governed, in fact, of all the reactions between human beings—of the entire web of life. As Sherrington has stated, "Environment drives the brain, the brain drives the various organs of the body," and here we believe we find the key to a mechanistic interpretation of all body processes.

On this basis we may see that the activities of life depend upon the ability of the parts of the body mechanism to respond adequately to adequate stimulation. This postulate applies not only to stimuli from visible forces, but to those received by the invasion of the micro-bodies which cause pyogenic or non-pyogenic infections. In the case of dangerous assaults by visible or invisible enemies, the brain, through the nerves and all parts of the motor mechanism, meets the attack by attempts at adaptation. Recovery, invalidism, and death depend upon the degree of success with which the attacking or invading enemies are met. Questions regarding disease become, therefore, questions in adaptation, and it is possible that, when studied in the light of this conception, the key to many hitherto unsolved physical problems may be found.

Perhaps no more convincing proof of our thesis may be secured than by a study of that ever-present phenomenon—*pain*. In whatever part of the body and by whatever apparent cause pain is produced, we find that it is invariably a stimulation to motor activity—whose ultimate object is protection. Thus by the muscular action resulting from pain we are protected against heat and cold; against too powerful light; against local anemia caused by prolonged pressure upon any portion of the body. So, too, pain of greater or less intensity compels the required emptying of the pregnant uterus and the evacuation of the intestine and the urinary bladder.

It should be noted that in every instance the muscular activity resulting from pain is specific in its type, its distribution, and its intensity, this specificity being true not only of pain which is the result of external stimulation, but also of the pain associated with certain types of infection.

*   *   *   *   *   *   *   *   *   *   *
*   *   *   *   *   *   *   *   *   *   *

Pain, however, is not the only symptom of the invasion of the body by pyogenic or parasitic organisms. Fever, invariably, and chills, often, accompany the course of the infections. Can these phenomena also be explained as adaptations of the motor mechanism for the good of the individual?

As the phenomena of chills and fever are most strikingly exhibited in malaria, let us study the course of events in that disease. It is known that the malarial parasite develops in the red blood-corpuscles, and that the chills and fever appear when the cycle of parasitic development is complete and the adults are ready to escape from the corpuscles of the blood plasma. Bass, of New Orleans, has proved that the favorable temperature for the growth of the malarial organism is 98°, and that at 102° the adult organisms will be killed, though the latter temperature is not fatal to the spores. The adult life of the malarial parasite begins after its escape into the blood plasma, and it is there that the organism is most susceptible to high temperature. We must infer, therefore, that the fever is an adaptation on the part of the host for despatching the enemy.

What, then, may be the protective part played by the

chill?   A chill is made up of intermittent contractions of all
the external muscles of the body.   This activity results in
an increase of the body heat and in an anemia of the superficial parts of the body, so that less heat can be lost by radia-
tion.   By this means, therefore, the external portions of the
body contribute measurably to the production of the beneficent and saving fever.

It must be remembered that this power of adaptation is
not peculiar to man alone, but that it is a quality shared by
all living creatures.   While the human body has been adapting itself for self-protection by producing a febrile reaction
whereby to kill the invading organisms, the invaders on their
side have been adapting themselves for a life struggle within
the body of the host.   In these mortal conflicts between
invaders and host, therefore, the issue is often in doubt, and
sometimes one and sometimes the other will emerge victori-
ous.

We must believe that a similar adaptive response exists in
all parasitic infections—the cycles varying according to the
stages in the development of the invaders.   If the bacteria
develop continuously, the fever is constant instead of intermittent, since the adequate stimulus is constantly present.

Bacteriology has taught us that both heat and cold are
fatal to pathogenic infections; for this reason either of the
apparently contradictory methods of treatment may help,
i. e., either hot or cold applications.   It should be borne in
mind, however, that we have to deal not only with the adult
organisms, but with the spores also.   The application of
cold may keep the spores from developing, while heat may
promote their development, and the course of the disease
may vary, therefore, according to our choice of treatment.

From this viewpoint, we can understand the intermittent temperature in a patient who is convalescing from an extreme infection, as peritonitis, pylephlebitis, multiple abscess of the liver, etc.   In these conditions there may occur days of normal temperature, followed by an abrupt rise which will last for several days—this in turn succeeded by another remittance.   This cycle may be repeated several times, and on our hypothesis we may believe it is caused by the successive development to maturity of spores of varying ages.

If these premises are sound, the wisdom of reducing the temperature in case of infection may well be questioned.

On this mechanistic basis the emotions also may be explained as activations of the entire motor mechanism for fighting, for escaping, for copulating.

*   *   *   *   *   *   *   *   *   *   *
*   *   *   *   *   *   *   *   *   *   *

The emotions, then, are the preparation for phylogenetic activities (Fig. 48).   If the activities were consummated, the fuel—glycogen—and the activating secretions from the thyroid, the adrenals, the hypophysis, would be consumed. In the activation without action these products must be eliminated as waste products and so a heavy strain is put upon the organs of elimination.   It is obvious that the body under emotion might be clarified by active muscular exercise, but the subject of the emotion is so strongly integrated thereby that it is difficult for him to engage in diverting, clarifying exertion.

*   *   *   *   *   *   *   *   *   *   *
*   *   *   *   *   *   *   *   *   *   *

So, as we have indicated already, certain deleterious effects
11

are produced when the body mechanism is activated without resultant action. For example, the output of adrenalin is increased, and, as a consequence, arteriosclerosis and cardio-

FIG. 48.—VIOLENT EFFORT.

The identity of the muscular activation which is called forth by extreme muscular exertion with that called forth by intense emotion is illustrated by the facial expression of this model, sculptured from life by Dr. R. Tait McKenzie, of the University of Pennsylvania. This model and those in Fig. 52 were made after a careful study of athletes at the moment of supreme effort. (Photo by H. D. Jones, from Underwood and Underwood, N. Y.)

vascular disease may occur in persons who have been subjected to prolonged emotional strain, since it has been proved that the prolonged administration of adrenalin will cause these conditions. We have stated that the emotions cause increased output of glycogen. Glycogen is a step toward diabetes, and therefore this disease, too, is prone to appear in persons under emotional strain. It is most common in those races which are especially emotional in character, so we are not surprised to find it especially prevalent among Jews. So common is this particular result of prolonged emotion that some one has said, "When the stocks go down in New York, diabetes goes up." Nephritis, also, may result from emotional stress, because of the strain put upon the kidneys by the unconsumed activating substances. The increased heart action and the presence of these activating secretions may cause myocarditis and heart degeneration. Claudication also may result from the impaired circulation.

The emotions may cause an inhibition of the digestive secretions and of intestinal peristalsis. This means that the digestive processes are arrested, that putrefaction and autointoxication will result, and that still further strain will thus be put upon the organs of elimination. Who has not observed in himself and in others when under the influence of fear, anger, jealousy, or grief that the digestive processes and general well-being are rapidly and materially altered; while as tranquillity, peace, and happiness return the physical state improves accordingly?

Dentists testify that as a result of continued strong emotion the character of the saliva changes, pyorrhea develops, and the teeth decay rapidly. Every one knows that strong emotion may cause the hair to fall out and to become prematurely gray.

As to the most important organ of all—the brain—every one is conscious of its impaired efficiency under emotional strain, and laboratory researches show that the deficiency is accounted for by actual cell deterioration; so the individual who day by day is under heavy emotional strain finds himself losing strength slowly—especially do his friends note it. By summation of stimuli his threshold becomes lowered until stimuli, which under normal conditions would be of no effect, produce undue responses. "The grasshopper becomes a burden," and prolonged rest and change of environmental conditions are necessary for restoration.

If in a long emotional strain the brain is beaten down; if the number of "low-efficiency" cells increases, the driving power of the brain is correspondingly lessened and therefore the various organs of the body may escape through the very inefficiency of the brain to produce in them forced activity. On the other hand, if the brain remains vigorous, the kidneys may take the strain and break down; if the kidneys do not break, the blood-vessels may harden; if the blood-vessels are not affected, the thyroid may become hyperplastic and produce Graves' disease; if the thyroid escapes, diabetes may develop; while if the iron constitution of the mechanism can successfully bear the strain in all its parts, then the individual will break his competitors, and their mechanisms will suffer in the struggle.

This whole train of deleterious results of body activation without action may be best observed and studied in that most emotional of diseases—exophthalmic goiter. In this disease the constantly stimulated distance ceptors dispossess the contact ceptors from the common path, and drive the motor mechanism to its own destruction, and the patient has the appearance of a person in great terror, or of a runner approaching the end of a Marathon race (Figs. 16 and 48 to 54).

Exophthalmic goiter may result from long emotional or

mental stress in those cases in which the thyroid takes the brunt of the strain upon the mechanism. As adrenalin increases blood-pressure, so thyroid secretion increases brain activity, and increased brain activity in turn causes an increased activation of the motor mechanism as a whole.

We know that a deficiency or lack of thyroid secretion will inhibit sexual emotion and conception; will produce

FIG. 49.—RUNNERS AT FINISH OF FOUR-MILE RACE.
Two show the typical facies of fear; the third, that of exhaustion.

stupidity and inertia; will diminish vitality. On the other hand, excessive thyroid secretion drives the entire mechanism at top speed; the emotions are intensified; the skin becomes soft and moist, the eyes are brilliant and staring; the limbs tremble; the heart pounds loudly and its pulsations often are visible; the respiration is rapid; the stimulation of the fear mechanism causes the eyes to protrude (Fig. 16); the temperature mounts at every slight provocation and may reach the incredible height of 110° even. In time, the entire organism is destroyed—literally consumed—by the concentration of dynamic energy. It is

Fig. 50.—Winner of Two-mile Relay Race.
The expression is like that of anger or pain about to change to that of exhaustion. (Photo by Underwood and Underwood, N. Y.)

interesting to note that in these patients emotion gains complete possession of the final common path; they are wild and delirious—but they never have pain.

All the diseases caused by excessive motor activity may

be called kinetic diseases.   Against the conditions in life
which produce them man reacts in various ways.   He intro-

FIG. 51.—CROSS-COUNTRY RACE.
Winner of six-mile cross-country race showing typical expression of exhaustion.   (Copyright by Underwood and Underwood, N. Y.)

duces restful variety into his life by hunting and fishing; by
playing golf and tennis; by horseback riding; by cultivating
hobbies which effectually turn the current of his thoughts

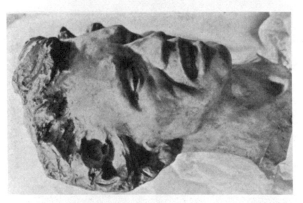

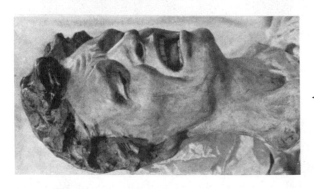

FIG. 52.—HEADS OF ATHLETES MODELED BY DR. R. TAIT MCKENZIE, OF THE UNIVERSITY OF PENNSYLVANIA. A, Breathlessness; B, fatigue; and C, exhaustion. See note to Fig. 48. (Photo by H. D. Jones, from Underwood and Underwood, N. Y.)

Fig. 53.—A Classic Conception of Fatigue—Phidippides, the First Marathon Runner.

"Athens is saved!"—Phidippides dies in the shout for his meed.—Browning.

169

from the consuming stress and strain of his business or professional life. These diversions are all rational attempts to relieve tension by self-preservative reactions. For the same reason man attempts to relieve the strain of contention with

FIG. 54.—A MODERN MARATHON RUNNER. (Copyright by Underwood and Underwood, N. Y.)

his fellow-man by unions, trusts, corporations. In spite of all efforts, however, many constitutions are still broken daily in the fierce conflicts of competition. We know how often the overdriven individual endeavors to minimize the activities of his motor mechanism by the use of agents which diminish brain activity, such as alcohol, tobacco, and various narcotics. Occasionally also, some person, who can find no respite from his own relentless energies, seeks relief in oblivion by suicide.

Most fortunately, two fundamental instincts—self-preservation and the propagation of the species—act powerfully to prevent this last fatal result, and instead the harassed individual seeks from others the aid which is lacking within himself. He may turn to the priest who seeks and often secures the final common path for faith in an over-ruling Providence, a faith which in many incontrovertible instances has proved sufficient in very truth to move mountains of lesser stimuli; or he turns to a physician, who too often treats the final outcome of the hyperactivity only. The physician who accepts the theory of the kinetic diseases, however, will not only repair as far as he may the lesions caused by the disordered and forced activities, but will, by compelling and forceful suggestion, secure the final common path for right conduct, that is, for a self- and species-preservative course of action as opposed to wrong conduct—a self- and species-destructive course of action.

By forcefully imparting to his patient the knowledge of the far-reaching effects of protracted emotional strain, of overwork, and of worry, the physician will automatically raise his threshold to the damaging activating stimuli which have produced the evil results. Even though some parts of his organism may have been permanently disabled, a patient thus protected may yet rise to a plane of poise and efficiency far above that of his uncontrolled fellows.

In extreme cases it does not seem unreasonable to believe that the uncontrolled patient might be rescued by the same principle which has proved effective in saving patients from the emotional and traumatic strain of surgical operations— the principle of anoci-association. That is, by disconnecting one or more of the activating organs from the brain, the motor mechanism might be saved from its self-destruction.

Under this hypothesis, that man in disease, as in health, is the product of his phylogeny as well as of ontogeny, the sphere of the physician's activities takes on new aspects of far-reaching and inspiring significance. Prognosis will become definite in proportion to the physician's knowledge not only of the ontogenetic history of the individual patient, but also of the phylogenetic history of the race. As that knowledge increases, as he appreciates more and more keenly the significance of environment in its effect upon individual development, in so far will the physician be in a position to contribute mightily to the welfare of the race.

THE KINETIC SYSTEM *

In this paper I formulate a theory which I hope will harmonize a large number of clinical and experimental data, supply an interpretation of certain diseases, and show by what means many diverse causes produce the same end effects.

Even should the theory prove ultimately to be true, it will in the mean time doubtless be subjected to many alterations. The specialized laboratory worker will, at first, fail to see the broader clinical view, and the trained clinician may hesitate to accept the laboratory findings. Our viewpoint has been gained from a consideration of both lines of evidence on rather a large scale.

The responsibility for the kinetic theory is assumed by myself, while the responsibility for the experimental data is shared fully by my associates, Dr. J. B. Austin, Dr. F. W. Hitchings, Dr. H. G. Sloan, and Dr. M. L. Menten.†

Introduction

The self-preservation of man and kindred animals is effected through mechanisms which transform latent energy into kinetic energy to accomplish adaptive ends. Man appropriates from environment the energy he requires in the

* Address delivered before the New York State Medical Society, April 28, 1914, to which has been added a further note regarding studies of hydrogen ion concentration in the blood.

† From H. K. Cushing Laboratory of Experimental Medicine, Western Reserve University, Cleveland.

form of crude food which is refined by the digestive system; oxygen is taken to the blood and carbon dioxid is taken from the blood by the respiratory system; to and from the myriads of working cells of the body, food and oxygen and waste are carried by the circulatory system; the body is cleared of waste by the urinary system; procreation is accomplished through the genital system; but none of these systems was evolved primarily for the purpose of transforming potential energy into kinetic energy for specific ends. Each system transforms such amounts of potential into kinetic energy as are required to perform its specific work; but no one of them transforms latent into kinetic energy for the purposes of escaping, fighting, pursuing, nor for combating infection. The stomach, the kidneys, the lungs, the heart strike no physical blow—their rôle is to do certain work to the end that the blow may be struck by another system evolved for that purpose. I propose to offer evidence that there is in the body a system evolved primarily for the transformation of latent energy into motion and into heat. This system I propose to designate "The Kinetic System."

The kinetic system does not directly circulate the blood, nor does it exchange oxygen and carbon dioxid; nor does it perform the functions of digestion, urinary elimination, and procreation; but though the kinetic system does not directly perform these functions, it does play indirectly an important rôle in each, just as the kinetic system itself is aided indirectly by the other systems.

The principal organs which comprise the kinetic system are the brain, the thyroid, the adrenals, the liver, and the muscles. The brain is the great central battery which drives the body; the thyroid governs the conditions favoring tissue oxidation; the adrenals govern immediate oxidation processes; the liver fabricates and stores glycogen; and the muscles are the great converters of latent energy into heat and motion.

Adrenalin alone, thyroid extract alone, brain activity alone, and muscular activity alone are capable of causing the body temperature to rise above the normal. The functional activity of no other gland of the body alone, and the secretion of no other gland alone, can cause a comparable rise in body temperature—that is, neither increased functional activity nor any active principle derived from the kidney, the liver, the stomach, the pancreas, the hypophysis, the parathyroids, the spleen, the intestines, the thymus, the lymphatic glands, or the bones can, *per se*, cause a rise in the general body temperature comparable to the rise that may be caused by the activity of the brain or the muscles, or by the injection of adrenalin or thyroid extract. Then, too, when the brain, the thyroid, the adrenals, the liver, or the muscles are eliminated, the power of the body to convert latent into kinetic energy is impaired or lost. I shall offer evidence tending to show that an excess of either internal or external environmental stimuli may modify one or more organs of the kinetic system, and that this modification may cause certain diseases. For example, alterations in the efficiency of the cerebral link may yield neurasthenia, mania, dementia; of the thyroid link, Graves' disease, myxedema; of the adrenal link, Addison's disease, cardiovascular disease.

This introduction may serve to give the line of our argument. We shall now consider briefly certain salient facts which relate to the conversion of latent into kinetic energy as an adaptive reaction. The experimental data are so many that they will later be published in a monograph.

The amount of latent energy which may be converted into kinetic energy for adaptive ends varies in different species, in individuals of the same species, in the same individual in different seasons; in the life cycle of growth, reproduction and decay; in the waking and sleeping hours; in disease and in activity. We shall here consider briefly the reasons for some of those variations and the mechanisms which make them possible.

Biologic Consideration of the Adaptive Variation in Amounts of Energy Stored in Various Animals

Energy is appropriated from the physical forces of nature that constitute the environment. This energy is stored in the body in quantities in excess of the needs of the moment. In some animals this excess storage is greater than in other animals. Those animals whose self-preservation is dependent on purely mechanical or chemical means of defense—such animals as crustaceans, porcupines, skunks or cobras—have a relatively small amount of convertible (adaptive) energy stored in their bodies. On the contrary, the more an animal is dependent on its muscular activity for self-preservation, the more surplus available (adaptive) energy there is stored in its body. It may be true that all animals have approximately an equal amount per kilo of chemical energy—but certainly they have not an equal amount stored in a form which is available for immediate conversion for adaptive ends.

Adaptive Variation in the Rate of Energy Discharge

What chance for survival would a skunk have without odor; a cobra without venom; a turtle without carapace; or a porcupine shorn of its barbs, in an environment of powerful and hostile carnivora? And yet in such an hostile environment many unprotected animals survive by their muscular power of flight alone. It is evident that the provision for the storage of "adaptive" energy is not the only evolved characteristic which relates to the energy of the body. The more the self-preservation of the animal depends on motor activity, the greater is the range of variation in the rate of discharge of energy. The rate of energy discharge is especially high in animals evolved along the line of hunter and hunted, such as the carnivora and the herbivora of the great plains.

Influences That Cause Variation in the Rate of Output of Energy in the Individual

Not only is there a variation in the rate of output of energy among various species of animals, but one finds also variations in the rate of output of energy among individuals of the same species. If our thesis that men and animals are mechanisms responding to environmental stimuli be correct, and further, if the speed of energy output be due to changes in the activating organs as a result of adaptive stimulation, then we should expect to find physical changes in the activating glands during the cycles of increased activation. What are the facts? We know that most animals have breeding seasons evolved as adaptations to the food supply and weather. Hence there is in most animals a mating season

12

in advance of the season of maximum food supply so that the
young may appear at the period when food is most abundant.
In the springtime most birds and mammals mate, and in the
springtime at least one of the great activating glands is
enlarged—the thyroid in man and in animals shows seasonal
enlargement.   The effect of the increased activity is seen
in the song, the courting, the fighting, in the quickened pulse,
and in a slightly raised temperature.   Even more activation
than that connected with the season is seen in the physical
state of mating, when the thyroid is known to enlarge
materially, though this increased activity, as we shall show
later, is probably no greater than the increased activity of
other activating glands.   In the mating season the kinetic
activity is speeded up; in short, there exists a state—a
fleeting state—of mild Graves' disease.   In the early stages
of Graves' disease, before the destructive phenomena are
felt, the kinetic speed is high, and life is on a sensuous edge.
Not only is there a seasonal rhythm to the rate of flow of
energy, but there is a diurnal variation—the ebb is at night,
and the full tide in the daytime.   This observation is verified
by the experiments which show that certain organs in the
kinetic chain are histologically exhausted, the depleted cells
being for the most part restored by sleep.

We have seen that there are variations in speed in different
species, and that in the same species speed varies with the
season of the year and with the time of day.   In addition
there are variations also in the rate of discharge of energy
in the various cycles of the life of the individual.   The young
are evolved at high speed for growth, so that as soon as
possible they may attain to their own power of self-defense;
they must adapt themselves to innumerable bacteria, to

food, and to all the elements in their external environment. Against their gross enemies the young are measurably protected by their parents; but the parents—except to a limited extent in the case of man—are unable to assist in the protection of the young against infectious disease.

The cycle of greatest kinetic energy for physiologic ends is the period of reproduction. In the female especially there is a cycle of increased activity just prior to her development into the procreative state. During this time secondary sexual characters are developed—the pelvis expands, the ovaries and the uterus grow rapidly, the mammary glands develop. Again in this period of increasing speed in the expenditure of energy we find the thyroid, the adrenals, and the hypophysis also in rapid growth. Without the normal development of the ovary, the thyroid, and the hypophysis, neither the male nor the female can develop the secondary sexual characters, nor do they develop sexual desire nor show seasonal cycles of activity, nor can they procreate. The secondary sexual characters—sexual desire, fertility— may be developed at will, for example, by feeding thyroid products from alien species to the individual deprived of the thyroid.

At the close of the child-bearing period there is a permanent diminution of the speed of energy discharge, for energy is no longer needed as it was for the self-preservation of the offspring before adolescence, and for the propagation of the species during the procreative period. Unless other factors intervene, this reduction in speed is progressive until senescent death. The diminished size of the thyroid of the aged bears testimony to the part the activating organs bear in the general decline.

We have now referred to variations in the rate of discharge of energy in different species; in individuals of the same species; in cycles in the same individual—such as the seasons of food supply, the periods of wakefulness and of sleep, the procreative period, and we have spoken of those variations caused artificially by thyroid feeding, thus far having confined our discussion to the conversion for adaptive purposes of latent into kinetic energy in muscular and in procreative action. We shall now consider the conversion of latent into kinetic energy in the production of heat,* and endeavor to answer the questions which arise at once: Is there one mechanism for the conversion of latent energy into heat and another mechanism for its conversion into muscular action? What is the adaptive advantage of fever in infection?

The Purpose and the Mechanism of Heat Production in Infections

Vaughan has shown that the presence in the body of any alien protein causes an increased production of heat, and that there is no difference between the production of fever by foreign proteins and by infections. Before the day of the hypodermic needle and of experimental medicine, the foreign proteins found in the body outside the alimentary tract were brought in by invading microörganisms. Such organisms interfered with and destroyed the host. The body, therefore, was forced to evolve a means of protection against these hostile organisms. The increased metabolism and fever in infection might operate as a protection in two ways—the increased fever, by interfering with bacterial growth, and the

---

* We use the terms "heat" and "muscular action" in the popular sense, though physicists use them to designate one and the same kind of energy.

increased metabolism, by breaking up the bacteria. Bacteriologists have taught us that bacteria grow best at the normal temperature of the body, hence fever must interfere with bacterial growth. With each rise of one degree centigrade the chemical activity of the body is increased 10 per cent. In acute infections there is aversion to food and frequently there is vomiting. In fever, then, we have diminished intake of energy, but an increased output of energy—hence the available potential energy in the body is rapidly consumed. This may be an adaptation for the purpose of breaking up the foreign protein molecules composing the bacteria. Thus the body may be purified by a chemical combustion so furious that frequently the host itself is destroyed. The problems of immunity are not considered here.

As to the mechanism which produces fever, we postulate that it is the same mechanism as that which produces muscular activity. Muscular activity is produced by the conversion of latent energy into motion, and fever is produced largely in the muscles by the conversion of latent energy into heat. We should, therefore, find similar changes in the brain, the adrenals, the thyroid, and the liver, whatever may be the purpose of the conversion of energy—whether for running, for fighting, for the expression of emotion, or for combating infection.

We shall first present experimental and clinical evidence which tends to show what part is played by the brain in the production of both muscular and febrile action, and later we shall discuss the parts played by the adrenals, the thyroid, and the liver.

Histologic Changes in the Brain-cells in Relation to the Maintenance of Consciousness and to the Production of the Emotions, Muscular Activity, and Fever

We have studied the brain-cells in human cases of fever, and in animals after prolonged insomnia; after the injection of the toxins of gonococci, of streptococci, of staphylococci, and of colon, tetanus, diphtheria, and typhoid bacilli; and after the injection of foreign proteins, of indol and skatol, of leucin, and of peptones. We have studied the brains of animals which had been activated in varying degrees up to the point of complete exhaustion by running, by fighting, by rage and fear, by physical injury, and by the injection of strychnin (Figs. 2, 4, 5, and 37). We have studied the brains of salmon at the mouth of the Columbia River and at its headwater (Fig. 55); the brains of electric fish, the storage batteries of which had been partially discharged, and of those the batteries of which had been completely discharged; the brains of woodchucks in hibernation and after fighting; the brains of humans who had died from anemia resulting from hemorrhage, from acidosis, from eclampsia, from cancer and from other chronic diseases (Figs. 40 to 43, 56, 74, and 75). We have studied also the brains of animals after the excision of the adrenals, of the pancreas, and of the liver (Figs. 57 and 60).

In every instance the loss of vitality—that is, the loss of the normal power to convert potential into kinetic energy— was accompanied by physical changes in the brain-cells (Figs. 45 and 46). The converse was also true, that is, the brain-cells of animals with normal vital power showed no histologic changes. The changes in the brain-cells were

identical whatever the cause. The crucial question then
becomes: Are these constant changes in the brain-cells the
result of work done by the brain-cells in running, in fighting,
in emotion, in fever? In other words, does the brain per-

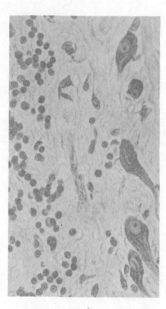

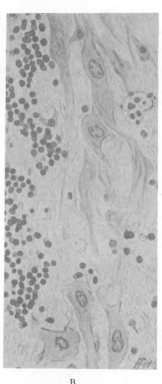

A

B

Area from Cerebellum of Male Salmon
from Ocean.

Area from Cerebellum of Male Salmon
from the River.

Fig. 55.—Exhaustion of Brain-cells of Salmon Caused by Expenditure
of Energy in Swimming from the Ocean to the Head Waters of
Columbia River. (Camera lucida drawings.)

form a definite rôle in the conversion of latent energy into
fever or into muscular action; or are the brain-cell changes
caused by the chemical products of metabolism? Happily,

Fig. 56.

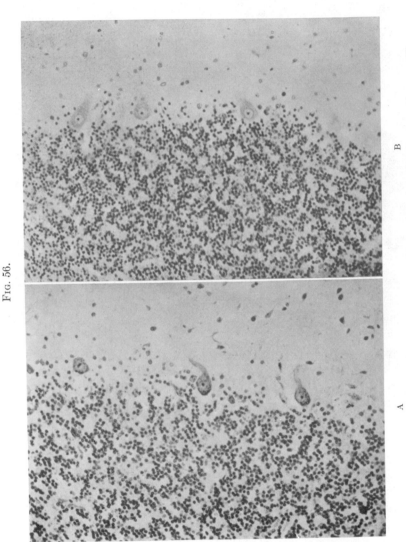

A
Section of Human Cerebellum—Normal
(× 310).

B
Section of Human Cerebellum Showing Effect
of Death from Eclampsia (× 310)

Note the hyperchromatic Purkinje cells.

Fig. 57.

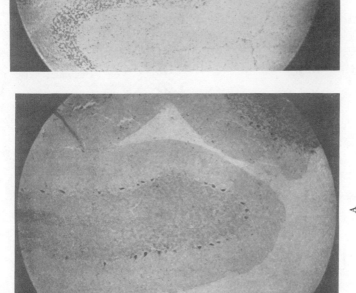

A

SECTION OF CEREBELLUM OF DOG—NORMAL

B

SECTION OF CEREBELLUM OF DOG AFTER HEPATECTOMY.

There is a general loss of cytoplasm and but faint traces of most of the Purkinje cells. This photograph presents striking evidence of the direct dependence of the brain upon the liver.

this crucial question was definitely answered by the following experiment: The circulations of two dogs were crossed in such a manner that the circulation of the head of one dog was anastomosed with the circulation of the body of another dog, and vice versa. A cord encircled the neck of each so firmly that the anastomosing circulation was blocked (Fig. 58). If the brain-cell changes were due to metabolic products, then when the body of dog "A" was injured, the

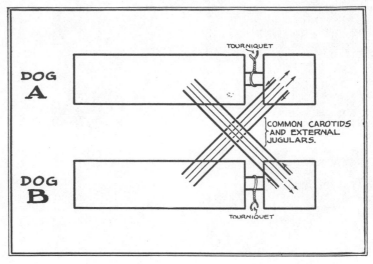

Fig. 58.—Schematic Drawing, showing Course of Blood-stream of Two Dogs with Eight-vessel Crossed Circulation.

brain of dog "A" would be normal and the brain of dog "B" would show changes. Our experiments showed brain-cell changes in the brain of the dog injured and no changes in the brain of the uninjured dog.

The injection of adrenalin causes striking brain-cell changes: first, a hyperchromatism, then a chromatolysis. Now if adrenalin caused these changes merely as a metabolic

phenomenon and not as a "work" phenomenon, then the
injection of adrenalin into the carotid artery of a crossed
circulation dog would cause no change in its circulation and
its respiration, since the brain thus injected is in exclusive
vascular connection with the body of another dog.   In our
experiment the blood-pressures of both dogs were recorded

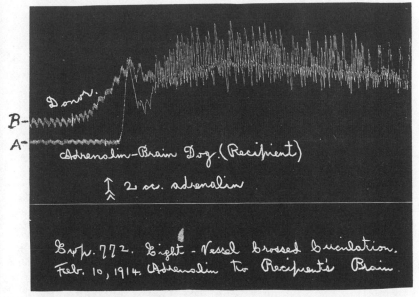

FIG. 59.—BLOOD-PRESSURE TRACING DEMONSTRATING THAT IN SPITE OF FACT
  THAT BLOOD OF DOG "A" PASSED THROUGH BRAIN OF DOG "B," YET
  BRAIN OF DOG "A" RECEIVED THE STIMULATION CAUSED BY INJECTION
  OF ADRENALIN INTO BLOOD OF DOG "A."

on a drum when adrenalin was injected into the common
carotid.   The adrenalin caused a rise in blood-pressure, an
increase in the force of cardiac contraction, increase in respiration, and a characteristic adrenalin rise in the blood-
pressure of both dogs.   The rise was seen first in the dog
whose brain alone received adrenalin and about a minute

later in the dog whose body alone received adrenalin (Fig. 59). Histologic examinations of the brains of both dogs showed marked hyperchromatism in the brain receiving adrenalin, while the brain receiving no adrenalin showed no change. Here is a clear-cut observation on the action of adrenalin on the brain, for both the functional and the histologic tests showed that adrenalin causes increased brain action. The significance of this affinity of the brain for adrenalin begins to be seen when I call attention to the following striking facts:

1. Adrenalin alone causes hyperchromatism followed by chromatolysis, and in overdosage causes the destruction of some brain-cells.

2. When both adrenal glands are excised and no other factor is introduced, the Nissl substance progressively disappears from the brain-cells until death. This far-reaching point will be taken up later (Fig. 60).

Here our purpose is to discuss the cause of the brain-cell changes. We have seen that in crossed brain and body circulation trauma causes changes in the cells of the brain which is disconnected from the traumatized body by its circulation, but which is connected with the traumatized body by the nervous system. We have seen that adrenalin causes activation of the body connected with its brain by the nervous system, and histologic changes in the brain acted on directly by the adrenalin, but we found no notable brain-cell changes in the other brain through which the products of metabolism have circulated.

In the foregoing we find direct evidence that the products of metabolism are not the principal cause of the brain-cell changes. We shall now present evidence to show that for

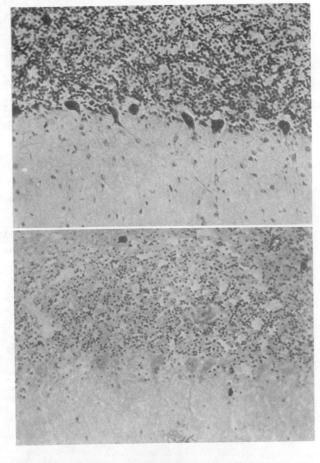

Fig. 60.

A

SECTION OF CEREBELLUM OF DOG—NORMAL
(× 310)

B

SECTION OF CEREBELLUM OF DOG SHOW-
ING EFFECT OF DOUBLE ADRENALEC-
TOMY (× 310).

The disastrous effect of the withdrawal of adrenalin from the system is marked by the depleted
cells. Every Purkinje cell shows signs of exhaustion, some are completely disintegrated. This and
the following photomicrograph (C) make evident
the dependence of the brain upon the adrenals.

C

SECTION OF CEREBELLUM OF DOG SHOW-
ING THE EFFECT ON THE BRAIN-CELLS
OF INJECTIONS OF ADRENALIN (× 310).

The remarkable activating effect of adrenalin is
strikingly shown by the intense hyperchromatism.

the most part the brain-cell changes are "work" changes. What work? We postulate that it is the work by which the energy stored in the brain-cells is converted into electricity or some other form of transmissible energy which then activates certain glands and muscles, thus converting latent energy into heat and motion. It has chanced that certain

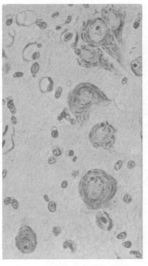 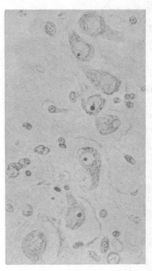

Area from Cerebellum of Electric
Fish—Normal.

Area from Cerebellum of Electric
Fish—Exhausted.

FIG. 61.—EXHAUSTION OF BRAIN-CELLS OF ELECTRIC FISH CAUSED BY EX-
PENDITURE OF ENERGY IN MAKING ELECTRIC DISCHARGES.

other studies have given an analogous and convincing proof of this postulate. In the electric fish a part of the muscular mechanism is replaced by a specialized structure for storing and discharging electricity. We found "work" changes in the brain-cells of electric fish after all their electricity had been rapidly discharged (Fig. 61). We found further that electric fish could not discharge their electricity when under anesthesia, and clinically we know that under deep morphin narcosis, and under anesthesia, the production both of heat and of muscular action is hindered. The action of morphin in lessening fever production is probably the result of its depressing influence on the brain-cells, because of which a diminished amount of their potential energy is converted into electricity and a diminished electric discharge from the brain to the muscles should diminish heat production proportionally. We found by experiment that under deep morphinization brain-cell changes due to toxins could be largely prevented (Fig. 62); in human patients deep morphinization diminishes the production of muscular action and of fever, and conserves life when it is threatened by acute infections. The contribution of the brain-cells to the production of heat is either the result of the direct conversion of their stored energy into heat, or of the conversion of their latent energy into electricity or a similar force, which in turn causes certain glands and muscles to convert latent energy into heat.

A further support to the postulate that the brain-cells contribute to the production of fever by sending impulses to the muscles is found in the effect of muscular exertion, or of other forms of motor stimulation, in the presence of a fever-producing infection. Under such circumstances muscular exertion causes additional fever, and causes also added but identical changes in the brain-cells. Thyroid extract and iodin have the same effect as muscular exertion and infection in the production of fever and the production of brain-cell changes. All this evidence is a strong argument in favor of the theory that certain constituents of the brain-cells

Fig. 62.

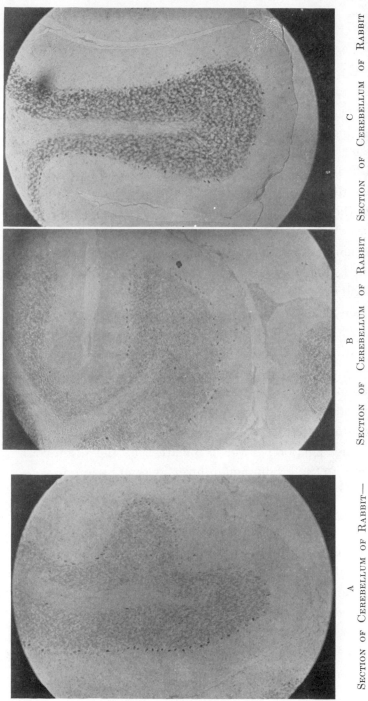

A
SECTION OF CEREBELLUM OF RABBIT—NORMAL (× 85).

B
SECTION OF CEREBELLUM OF RABBIT SHOWING EFFECT OF DIPHTHERIA TOXIN (× 85).
Note the general hypochromatism.

C
SECTION OF CEREBELLUM OF RABBIT SHOWING EFFECT OF DIPHTHERIA TOXIN *Plus Morphin* (× 85).
The protective effect of morphin is illustrated by the large percentage of hyperchromatic cells.

192

are consumed in the work performed by the brain in the production of fever.

That the stimulation of the brain-cells without gross activity of the skeletal muscles and without infection can produce heat is shown as follows:

(a) Fever is produced when animals are subjected to fear without any consequent exertion of the skeletal muscles.

(b) The temperature of the anxious friends of patients

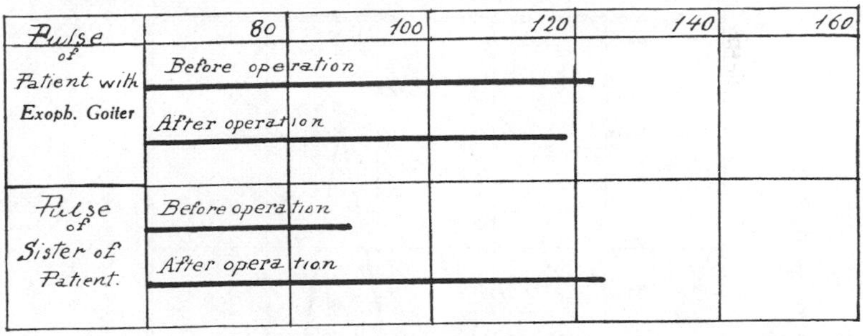

Pulse	80	100	120	140	160
of Patient with	Before operation				
Exoph. Goiter	After operation				
Pulse of	Before operation				
Sister of Patient	After operation				

FIG. 63.—CHART ILLUSTRATING PROTECTION AFFORDED BY USE OF *Anociassociation* IN THYROIDECTOMY.

The patient's brain received neither traumatic nor psychic stimuli from the time she was anesthetized in bed until she returned again from the operating-room. Her pulse-rate *fell* slightly during the operation. On the other hand, the psychic strain undergone by the patient's sister while the operation was being performed caused her pulse-rate to rise to 124.

will rise while they await the outcome of an operation (Fig. 63).

(c) The temperature and pulse of patients will rise as a result of the mere anticipation of a surgical operation (Fig. 64).

(d) There are innumerable clinical observations as to the effect of emotional excitation on the temperature of patients. A rise of a degree or more is a common result of a visit from a tactless friend. There is a traditional Sunday increase of temperature in hospital wards. Now the visitor does not

13

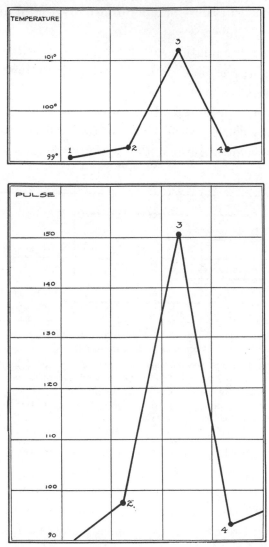

FIG. 64.—The patient, a foreigner, was brought to the operating-room from the accident ward. Pulse and temperature normal. When he found himself in the operating-room he was greatly disturbed. It was impossible to make him understand that his leg was not to be amputated but only a plaster cast applied. Under this stimulus his pulse rose to 150 and he soon developed a temperature of 101.2° F.

bring and administer more infection to the patient to cause
this rise, and the rise of temperature occurs even if the
patient does not make the least muscular exertion as a result
of the visit.   I once observed an average increase of one and
one-eighth degrees of temperature in a ward of fifteen children as a result of a Fourth of July celebration.

Is the contribution of the brain to the production of heat
due to the conversion of latent energy directly into heat, or
does the brain produce heat principally by converting its
latent energy into electricity or some similar form of transmissible energy which, through nerve connections, stimulates other organs and tissues, which in turn convert their
stores of latent energy into heat?

According to Starling, when the connection between the
brain and the muscles of an animal is severed by curare, by
anesthetics, by the division of the cord and nerves, then the
heat-producing power of the animal so modified is on a level
with that of cold-blooded animals.   With cold the temperature falls, with heat it rises.   Such an animal has no more
control over the conversion of latent energy into heat than
it has over the conversion of latent energy into motion.

Electric stimulation done over a period of time causes
brain-cell changes, and electric stimulation of the muscles
causes a rise in temperature.

Summary of Brain-cell Studies

In our crossed circulation experiments we found that
neither waste products nor metabolic poisons could be considered the principal cause of the brain-cell changes.   We
found that in the production both of muscular action and of
fever there were brain-cell changes which showed a quantita-

tive relation to the temperature changes or to the muscular work done. We observed that under deep morphinization the febrile response or the muscular work done was either diminished or eliminated and that the brain-cell changes were correspondingly diminished or eliminated. We found also that brain-cell changes and muscular work followed electric stimulation alone. I conclude, therefore, that the brain-cell changes are work changes.

We shall next consider other organs of the kinetic system in their relation to muscular activity, to emotion, to consciousness, to sleep, to hibernation, and to heat production.

The Adrenals

In our extensive study of the brain in its relation to the production of energy and the consequent exhaustion caused by fear and rage; by the injection of foreign proteins, of bacterial toxins, and of strychnin; by anaphylaxis; by the injection of thyroid extract, of adrenalin, and of morphin, we found that, with the exception of morphin, each of these agents produced identical changes in the brain-cells. As we believed that the adrenals were intimately associated with the brain in its activities, we concluded that the adrenals also must have been affected by each of these agents. To prove this relation, we administered the above-mentioned stimuli to animals and studied their effects upon the adrenals by functional, histologic, and surgical methods, the functional tests being made by Cannon's method.

Functional Study of the Adrenals.—Our method of applying the Cannon test for adrenalin was as follows: (a) The blood of the animals was tested before the application of the stimulus. If this test was negative, then (b) the stimulus was applied and the blood again tested. If this second test was negative, a small amount of adrenalin was added. If a positive reaction was then given, the negative result was accepted as conclusive. (c) If the control test was negative, then the stimulus was given. If the blood after stimulation gave a positive result for adrenalin, a second test of the same animal's blood was made twenty-five minutes or more later. If the second test was negative, then the positive result of the first test was accepted as conclusive.

We have recorded 66 clear-cut experiments on dogs, which show that after fear and rage, after anaphylaxis, after injections of indol and skatol, of leucin and creatin, of the toxins of diphtheria and colon bacilli, of streptococci and staphylococci, of foreign proteins, and of strychnin, the Cannon test for adrenalin was positive. The test was negative after trauma under anesthesia, and after intravenous injections of thyroid extract, of thyroglobin, and of the juices of various organs injected into the same animal from which the organs were taken. Placental extract gave a positive test. The test was sometimes positive after electric stimulation of the splanchnic nerves. On the other hand, if the nerve supply to the adrenals had been previously divided, or if the adrenals had been previously excised, then the Cannon test was negative after the administration of each of the foregoing adequate stimuli. Blood taken directly from the adrenal vein gave a positive result, but under deep morphinization the blood from the adrenal vein was negative, and under deep morphinization the foregoing adequate stimuli were negative.

In brief, the agencies that in our brain-cell studies were

found to cause hyperchromatism followed by chromatolysis gave positive results in the Cannon test for adrenalin (Fig. 62). The one agent which was found to protect the brain against changes in the Nissl substance—morphin—gave a negative result in the Cannon test for adrenalin. After excision of the adrenals, or after division of their nerve supply, all Cannon tests for adrenalin were negative.

Histologic Study of the Adrenals.—Histologic studies of the adrenals after the application of the adequate stimuli which gave positive results to the Cannon test for adrenalin are now in progress, and thus far the histologic studies corroborate the functional tests.

In hibernating woodchucks, the cells of the adrenal cortex were found to be vacuolated and shrunken. In one hundred hours of insomnia, in surgical shock, in strong fear, in exhaustion from fighting, after peptone injections, in acute infections, the adrenals undergo histologic changes characteristic of exhaustion (Figs. 66 to 67).

We have shown that brain and adrenal activity go hand in hand, that is, that the adrenal secretion activates the brain, and that the brain activates the adrenals. The fundamental question which now arises is this: Are the brain and the adrenals interdependent? A positive answer may be given to this question, for the evidence of the dependence of the brain upon the adrenals is as clear as is the evidence of the dependence of the adrenals upon the brain. (1) After excision of the adrenals, the brain-cells undergo continuous histologic and functional deterioration until death. During this time the brain progressively loses its power to respond to stimuli and there is also a progressive loss of muscular power and a diminution of body temperature. (2)

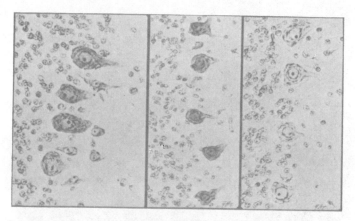

Cells from normal cerebellum. Cells from cerebellum showing the immediate results of injection of skatol. Note the hyperchromatism. Cells from cerebellum showing the late results of injection of skatol. Note the chromatolysis.

EFFECT ON BRAIN-CELLS OF SKATOL INJECTION. (Camera lucida drawings.)

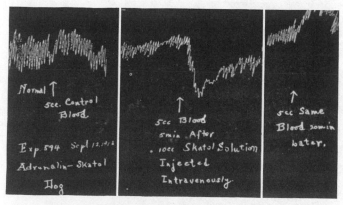

Cannon test for adrenalin, demonstrating the increased output of adrenalin after injection of skatol.

FIG. 65.—ACTIVATION OF KINETIC SYSTEM CAUSED BY INJECTION OF SKATOL. THESE ILLUS RATIONS INDICATE THE EXPLANATION OF THE GENERAL EXHAUSTION SHOWN IN CASES OF AUTO-INTOXICATION.

Fig. 66.

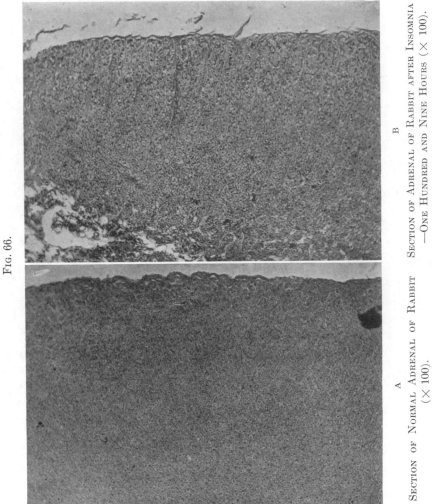

A

Section of Normal Adrenal of Rabbit (× 100).

B

Section of Adrenal of Rabbit after Insomnia —One Hundred and Nine Hours (× 100).

Note the vacuolated spaces and the general disappearance of cytoplasm in B.

FIG. 37.

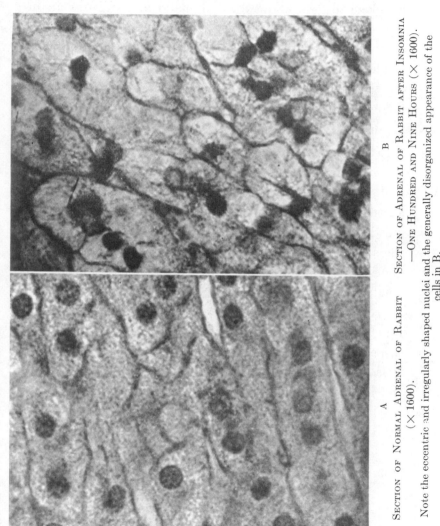

A

SECTION OF NORMAL ADRENAL OF RABBIT
(× 1600).

B

SECTION OF ADRENAL OF RABBIT AFTER INSOMNIA
—ONE HUNDRED AND NINE HOURS (× 1600).

Note the eccentric and irregularly shaped nuclei and the generally disorganized appearance of the
cells in B.

In our crossed circulation experiments we found that adrenalin alone could cause increased brain activity, while histologically we know that adrenalin alone causes an increase of the Nissl substance. An animal, both of whose adrenals had been excised, showed no hyperchromatism in the brain-cells after the injection of strychnin, toxins, foreign proteins, etc. (3) When the adrenal nerve supply is divided (Cannon-Elliott), then there is no increased adrenal activity in response to adequate stimuli.

From these studies we are forced to conclude not only that the brain and adrenals are interdependent, but that the brain is actually more dependent upon the adrenals than the adrenals upon the brain, since the brain deteriorates progressively to death without the adrenals, while the adrenal whose connection with the brain has been broken by the division of its nerve supply will still produce sufficient adrenalin to support life.

From the strong affinity of the brain-cells for adrenalin which was manifested in our experiments we may strongly suspect that the Nissl substance is a volatile, extremely unstable combination of certain elements of the brain-cells and adrenalin, because the adrenals alone do not take the Nissl stain and the brain deprived of adrenalin also does not take Nissl stain. The consumption of the Nissl substance in the brain-cells is lessened or prevented by morphin, as is the output of adrenalin; and the consumption of the Nissl substance is also lessened or prevented by nitrous oxid. But morphin does not prevent the action of adrenalin injected into the circulation, hence the control of morphin over energy expenditure is exerted directly on the brain-cells. Apparently morphin and nitrous oxid both act

FIG. 68.

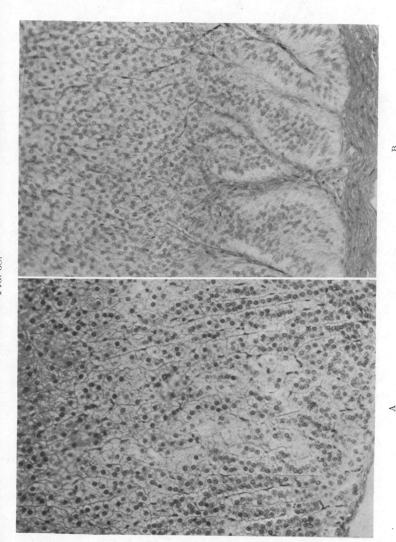

A

SECTION OF ADRENAL OF DOG. NORMAL (× 310).

B

SECTION OF ADRENAL OF DOG SHOWING EFFECT OF PROLONGED SHOCK AS EVIDENCED BY THE LOSS OF CYTOPLASM (× 310).

Adrenal of dog—normal and prolonged shock.

through this interference with oxidation in the brain. We, therefore, conclude that within a certain range of acidity of the blood adrenalin can unite with the brain-cells only through the mediation of oxygen, and that the combination of adrenalin, oxygen, and certain brain-cell constituents causes the electric discharge that produces heat and motion. In this interrelation of the brain and the adrenals we have what is, perhaps, the master key to the automatic action of the body. Through the special senses environmental stimuli reach the brain and cause it to liberate energy, which in turn activates certain other organs and tissues, among which are the adrenals. The increased output of adrenalin activates the brain to still greater activity, as a result of which again the entire sympathetic nervous system is further activated, as is manifested by increased heart action, more rapid respiration, raised blood-pressure, increased output of glycogen, increased power of the muscles to metabolize glucose, etc.

If this conclusion be well founded, we should find corroborative evidence in histologic changes in that great storehouse of potential energy, the liver, as a result of the application of each of the adequate stimuli which produced brain-cell and adrenal changes.

The Liver

Prolonged insomnia, prolonged physical exertion, infections, injections of toxins and of strychnin, rage and fear, physical injury under anesthesia, in fact, all the adequate stimuli which affected the brain and the adrenals, produced constant and identical histologic changes in the liver—the cells stained poorly, the cytoplasm was vacuolated, the nuclei were crenated, the cell membranes were irregular, the most marked changes occurring in the cells of the periphery of the lobules (Figs. 69 and 70). In prolonged insomnia the striking changes in the liver were repaired by one séance of sleep.

Are the histologic changes in the liver cells due to metabolism or toxic products, or are they "work" changes incident to the conversion of latent into kinetic energy? Are the brain, adrenals, and liver interdependent? The following facts establish the answers to these queries:

(1) The duration of life after excision of the liver is about the same as after adrenalectomy—approximately eighteen hours.

(2) The amount of glycogen in the liver was diminished in all the experiments showing brain-adrenal activity; and when the histologic changes were repaired, the normal amount of glycogen was again found.

(3) In crossed circulation experiments changes were found in the liver of the animal whose brain received the stimulus.

From these premises we must consider that the brain, the adrenals, and the liver are mutually dependent on one another for the conversion of latent into kinetic energy. Each is a vital organ, each equally vital. It may be said that excision of the brain may apparently cause death in less time than excision of the liver or adrenals, but this statement must be modified by our definition of death. If all the brain of an animal be removed by decapitation, its body may live on for at least eleven hours if its circulation be maintained by transfusion. An animal may live for weeks or months after excision of the cerebral hemispheres and the

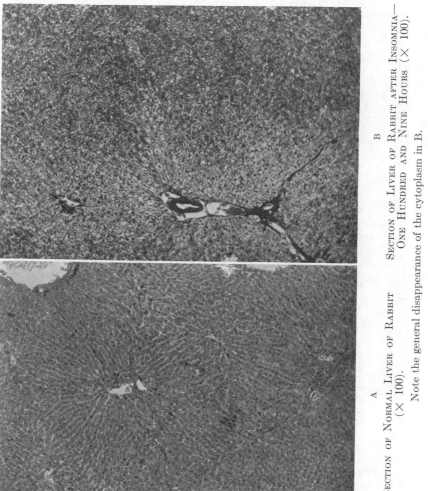

A

SECTION OF NORMAL LIVER OF RABBIT
(× 100).

B

SECTION OF LIVER OF RABBIT AFTER INSOMNIA—
ONE HUNDRED AND NINE HOURS (× 100).

Note the general disappearance of the cytoplasm in B.

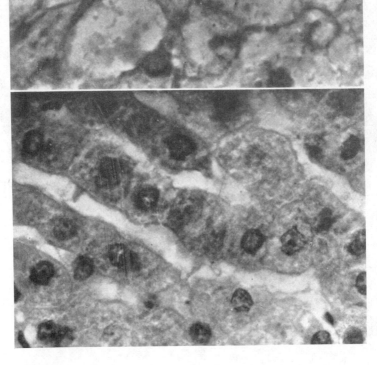

Fig. 70.

A
Section of Normal Liver of Rabbit
(× 1600).

B
Section of Liver of Rabbit after Insomnia—
One Hundred and Nine Hours (× 1600).

Note the disappearance of some nuclei in B and the misshapen and eccentric appearance of the
rest.

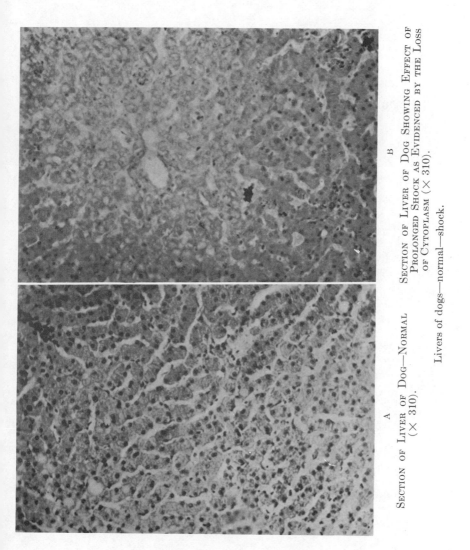

A

SECTION OF LIVER OF DOG—NORMAL
(× 310).

B

SECTION OF LIVER OF DOG SHOWING EFFECT OF
PROLONGED SHOCK AS EVIDENCED BY THE LOSS
OF CYTOPLASM (× 310).

Livers of dogs—normal—shock.

cerebellum, while an overtransfused animal may live many hours, days even, after the destruction of the medulla. It is possible even that the brain actually is a less vital organ than either the adrenals or the liver.

In our research to discover whether any other organs should be included with the brain, the adrenals, and the liver in this mutually interdependent relation, we hit upon an experiment which throws light upon this problem.

Groups of rabbits were gently kept awake for one hundred hours by relays of students, an experiment which steadily withdrew energy but caused not the slightest physical or emotional injury to any of them; no drug, toxin, or other agent was given to them; they were given sufficient food and drink. In brief, the internal and external environments of these animals were kept otherwise normal excepting for the gentle stimuli which insured continued wakefulness. This protracted insomnia gradually exhausted the animals completely, some to the point of death even. Some of the survivors were killed immediately after the expiration of one hundred hours of wakefulness, others after varying intervals.

Histologic studies were made of every tissue and organ in the body. Three organs, the brain, the adrenals, and the liver, and these three only, showed histologic changes. In these three organs the histologic changes were marked, and were almost wholly repaired by one séance of sleep. In each instance these histologic changes were identical with those seen after physical exertion, emotions, toxins, etc.* It

* Further studies have given evidence that the elimination of the acids resulting from energy-transformation as well as the conversion of energy stored in the kinetic organs causes histologic changes in the liver, the adrenals, and possibly in the brain.

would appear, then, that these three organs take the stress of life—the brain is the "battery," the adrenals the "oxydizer," and the liver the "gasoline tank." This clear-cut insomnia experiment corresponds precisely with our other brain-adrenal observations.

With these three kinetic organs we may surely associate also the "furnace," the muscles, in which the energy provided by the brain, adrenals, and liver, plus oxygen, is fabricated into heat and motion.

Benedict, in his monumental work on metabolism, has demonstrated that in the normal state, at least, variations in the heart-beat parallel variations in metabolism. He and others have shown also that all the energy of the body, whether evidenced by heat or by motion, is produced in the muscles. In the muscles, then, we find the fourth vital link in the kinetic chain. The muscles move the body, circulate the blood, effect respiration, and govern the body temperature. They are the passive servants of the brain-adrenal-liver syndrome.

Neither the brain, the adrenals, the liver, nor the muscles, however, nor all of these together, have the power to change the rate of the expenditure of energy; to make possible the increased expenditure in adolescence, in pregnancy, in courting, and mating, in infections. No one of these organs, nor all of them together, can act as a pace-maker or sensitizer. The brain acts immediately in response to the stimuli of the moment; the adrenals respond instantly to the fickle brain and the effects of their actions are fleeting; the liver contains fuel only and cannot activate, and the muscles in turn act as the great furnace in which the final transformation into available energy is made.

The Thyroid

Another organ—the thyroid—has the special power of governing the *rate of discharge* of energy; in other words, the thyroid is the pace-maker.   Unfortunately, the thyroid cannot be studied to advantage either functionally or histologically, for there is as yet no available test for thyroid secretion in the blood as there is for adrenalin, and thyroid activity is not attended by striking histologic changes. Therefore the only laboratory studies which have been satisfactory thus far are those by which the iodin content of the thyroid has been established.   Iodin is stored in the colloid lacunæ of the thyroid and, in combination with certain proteins, is the active agent of the thyroid.

Beebe has shown that electric stimulation of the nerve supply of the thyroid diminishes the amount of iodin which it contains, and it is known that in the hyperactive thyroid in Graves' disease the iodin content is diminished.   The meagerness of laboratory studies, however, is amply compensated by the observations which the surgeon has been able to make on a vast scale—observations which are as definite as are the results of laboratory experiments.

The brain-cells and the adrenals are securely concealed from the eye of the clinician, hence the changes produced in them by different causes escape his notice, but the thyroid has always been closely scrutinized by him.   The clinician knows that every one of the above-mentioned causes of increased brain-cell, adrenal, liver and muscle activity may cause an increase in the activity of both the normal or the enlarged thyroid; and he knows only too well that in a given case of exophthalmic goiter the same stimuli which excite the brain, the adrenals, the liver, and the muscles to increased activity will also aggravate this disease.

The function of the thyroid in the kinetic chain is best evidenced, however, by its rôle in the production of fever. Fever results from the administration of thyroid extract alone in large doses. In the hyperactivity of the thyroid in exophthalmic goiter one sees a marked tendency to fever; in severe cases there is daily fever. In fact, in Graves' disease we find displayed to an extraordinary degree an exaggeration of the whole action of the kinetic mechanism.

We have stated that in acute Graves' disease there is a tendency to the production of spontaneous fever, and that there is a magnified diurnal variation in temperature which is due to an increased output of energy in even the normal reaction producing consciousness. In Graves' disease there is, therefore, a state of intensified consciousness, which is associated with low brain thresholds to all stimuli—both to stimuli that cause muscular action and to stimuli that cause fever. The intensity of the kinetic discharge is seen in the constant fine tremor. It is evident that the thresholds of the brain have been sensitized. In this hypersensitization we find the following strong evidence as to the identity of the various mechanisms for the production of fever. In the state of superlative sensitization which is seen in Graves' disease we find that the stimuli that produce muscular movement, the stimuli that produce emotional phenomena, and the stimuli that produce fever are as nearly as can be ascertained equally effective. Clinical evidence regarding this point is abundant, for in patients with Graves' disease we find that the three types of conversion of energy resulting from emotional stimulation, from infection stimulation, and from nociceptor stimulation (pain), are, as nearly as can be judged, equally exaggerated. In the acute cases of Graves' disease the explosive conversion of latent energy into heat and motion is unexcelled by any other known normal or pathologic phenomenon. Excessive thyroid secretion, as in thyrotoxicosis from functioning adenomata, and excessive thyroid feeding, cause all the phenomena of Graves' disease except the exophthalmos and the emotional facies (Figs. 15 and 23). The ligation of arteries, the division of its nerve supply, or the excision of part of the gland, may reverse the foregoing picture and restore the normal condition. The patient notes the effect on the second day and often within a week is relatively quiescent. On the contrary, if there is thyroid deficiency there results the opposite state, a reptilian sluggishness.

At will, then, through diminished, normal, or excessive administration of thyroid secretion, we may produce an adynamic, a normal, or an excessively dynamic state. By the thyroid influence, the brain thresholds are lowered and life becomes exquisite; without its influence the brain becomes a globe of relatively inert substance. Excessive doses of iodin alone cause most of the symptoms of Graves' disease. As we have stated, the active constituent of the thyroid is iodin in a special protein combination which is stored in the colloidal spaces. Hence one would not expect to find changes in the cells of the thyroid gland as a result of increased activity unless it be prolonged.

We have thus far considered the normal rôles played by the brain, the adrenals the liver, the muscles, and the thyroid in transforming latent into kinetic energy in the form of heat and motion as an adaptive response to environmental st muli.

The argument may be strengthened, however, by the discussion of the effect of the impairment of any of these links in the kinetic chain upon the conversion of latent into kinetic energy.

Effect Upon the Output of Energy of Impaired or Lost Function of Each of the Several Links in the Kinetic Chain

(1) *The Brain.*—In cerebral softening we may find all the organs of the body comparatively healthy excepting the brain. As the brain is physically impaired it cannot normally stimulate other organs to the conversion of latent energy into heat or into motion, but, on the contrary, in these cases we find feeble muscular and intellectual power. I believe also that in patients with cerebral softening, infections such as pneumonia show a lower temperature range than in patients whose brains are normal.

(2) *The Adrenals.*—In such destructive lesions of the adrenals as Addison's disease one of the cardinal symptoms is a subnormal temperature and impaired muscular power. Animals upon whom double adrenalectomy has been performed show a striking fall in temperature, muscular weakness,—after adrenalectomy the animal may not be able to stand even,—and progressive chromatolysis.

(3) *The Liver.*—When the function of the liver is impaired by tumors, cirrhosis, or degeneration of the liver itself, then the entire energy of the body is correspondingly diminished. This diminution of energy is evidenced by muscular and mental weakness, by diminished response and by gradual loss of efficiency which finally reaches the state of asthenia.

(4) *The Muscles.*—It has been observed clinically that if the muscles are impaired by long disuse, or by a disease such

as myasthenia gravis, then the range of production of both
heat and motion is below normal.   This is in agreement with
the experimental findings that anesthetics, curare, or any
break in the muscle-brain connection causes diminished
muscular and heat production.

(5) *The Thyroid.*—In myxedema one of the cardinal
symptoms is a persistently subnormal temperature and,
though prone to infection, subjects of myxedema show but
feeble febrile response and readily succumb.   This clinical
observation is strikingly confirmed by laboratory observations; normal rabbits subjected to fear showed a rise in
temperature of from one to three degrees, while two rabbits
whose thyroids had been previously removed and who had
then been subjected to fright showed much less febrile
response.   Myxedema subjects show a loss of physical and
mental energy which is proportional to the lack of thyroid.
Deficiency in any of the organs of the kinetic chain causes
alike loss of heat, loss of muscular and emotional action, of
mental power, and of the power of combating infections—
the negative evidence thus strongly supports the positive.
By accumulating all the evidence we believe we are justified
in associating the brain, the adrenals, the thyroid, the
muscles, and the liver as vital links in the kinetic chain.
Other organs play a rôle undoubtedly, though a minor one.

Studies in Hydrogen Ion Concentration in Activation of the Kinetic System

Having established the identity of some, at least, of the
organs which constitute the kinetic chain, we endeavored to
secure still further evidence regarding the energy-trans-
forming function of these organs by making studies of the

H-ion concentration of the blood, as one would expect, *prima facie*, that the normal reaction would be altered by kinetic activation.*

H-ion concentration tests were made after the application of the adequate stimuli by which the function of the kinetic organs had been determined, and we studied also the effect upon the acidity of the blood of strychnin convulsions after destruction of the medulla; of deep narcotization with morphin before anesthesia; of deep narcotization with morphin after the H-ion concentration had already been increased by fear, by anger, by exertion, by injury under anesthesia, or by anesthesia alone.

The complete data of these experiments will be later reported in a monograph; here it is sufficient to state that anger, fear, injury, muscular exertion, inhalation anesthesia, strychnin, alcohol, in fact, all the stimuli which we had already found to produce histologic changes in the brain, the adrenals, and the liver—excepting bacterial toxins— caused increased H-ion concentration. Of striking significance is the fact that morphin alone caused no change in the H-ion concentration, while if administered before the application of a stimulus which by itself produced increased H-ion concentration, the action of that stimulus was neutralized or postponed. If, however, morphin was administered *after* increased acidity had been produced by any stimulus, or by inhalation anesthesia, then the time required for the restoration of the normal alkalinity was much prolonged, and in some instances the power of acid neutralization was permanently lost.

After excision of the liver, the normal H-ion concentration

* The H-ion observations were made in my laboratory by Dr. M. L. Menten.

was maintained for periods varying from one to several
hours, after which the concentration (acidity) began to
increase as the vitality of the animal began to decline, the
concentration (acidity) increasing rapidly until death.
After excision of the adrenals the blood remained normal
for from four to six hours, when the H-ion concentration
increased rather suddenly, the increase being synchronous
with the incidence of the phenomena which immediately
preceded death.

In none of these cases was it determined whether the increased H-ion concentration was due to other causes of
death or whether death was due to the increased acidity.

It is also significant that after the application of each of
the adequate stimuli which increased the H-ion concentration of the blood in other parts of the body the blood from
the adrenal vein showed a slight diminution in acidity, as,
in most instances, did the blood from the hepatic vein also.

In fact, the H-ion concentration of the blood in the adrenal
vein was less than in the blood of any other part of the circulation.

Kinetic Diseases

If our conclusions are sound, then in the kinetic system
we find an explanation of many diseases, and having found
the explanation, we may find new methods of combating
them.

When the kinetic system is driven at an overwhelming
rate of speed,—as by severe physical injury, by intense
emotional excitation, by perforation of the intestines, by
the pointing of an abscess into new territory, by the sudden
onset of an infectious disease, by an overdose of strychnin,

by a Marathon race, by a grilling fight, by foreign proteins, by anaphylaxis,—the result of these acute overwhelming activations of the kinetic system is clinically designated shock, and according to the cause is called traumatic shock, toxic shock, anaphylactic shock, drug shock, etc.

The essential pathology of shock is identical whatever the cause. If, however, instead of an intense overwhelming activation, the kinetic system is continuously or intermittently overstimulated through a considerable period of time, as long as each of the links in the kinetic chain takes the strain equally the result will be excessive energy conversion, excessive work done; but usually, under stress, some one link in the chain is unable to take the strain and then the evenly balanced work of the several organs of the kinetic system is disturbed. If the brain cannot endure the strain, then neurasthenia, nerve exhaustion, or even insanity follows. If the thyroid cannot endure the strain, it undergoes hyperplasia, which in turn may result in a colloid goiter or in exophthalmic goiter. If the adrenals cannot endure the strain, cardiovascular disease may develop. If the liver cannot take the strain, then death from acute acidosis may follow, or if the neutralizing effect of the liver is only partially lost, then the acidity may cause Bright's disease. Overactivation of the kinetic system may cause glycosuria and diabetes.

Identical physical and functional changes in the organs of the kinetic system may result from intense continued stimulation from any of the following causes: Excessive physical labor, athletic exercise, worry or anxiety, intestinal autointoxication, chronic infections, such as oral sepsis, tonsillitis, and adenoids; chronic appendicitis, chronic cholecystitis, colitis, and skin infections; the excessive intake of protein food (foreign protein reaction); emotional strain, pregnancy, stress of business or professional life—all of which are known to be activators of the kinetic system.

From the foregoing statements we are able to understand the muscular weakness following fever; we can understand why the senile have neither muscular power nor strong febrile reaction; why long-continued infections produce pathologic changes in the organs constituting the kinetic chain; why the same pathologic changes result from various forms of activation of the kinetic system. In this hypothesis we find a reason why cardiovascular disease may be caused by chronic infection, by auto-intoxication, by overwork, or by emotional excitation. We now see that the reason why we find so much difficulty in differentiating the numerous acute infections from each other is because they play upon the same kinetic chain. Our postulate harmonizes the pathologic democracy of the kinetic organs, for it explains not only why, in many diseases, the pathologic changes in these organs are identical, but why the same changes are seen as the result of emotional strain and overwork. We can thus understand how either emotional strain or acute or chronic infection may cause either exophthalmic goiter or cardiovascular disease; how chronic intestinal stasis with the resultant absorption of toxins may cause cardiovascular disease, neurasthenia, or goiter. Here is found an explanation of the phenomena of shock, whether the shock be the result of toxins, of infection, of foreign proteins, of anaphylaxis, of psychic stimuli, or of a surgical operation with its combination of both psychic and traumatic elements.

FIG. 72.

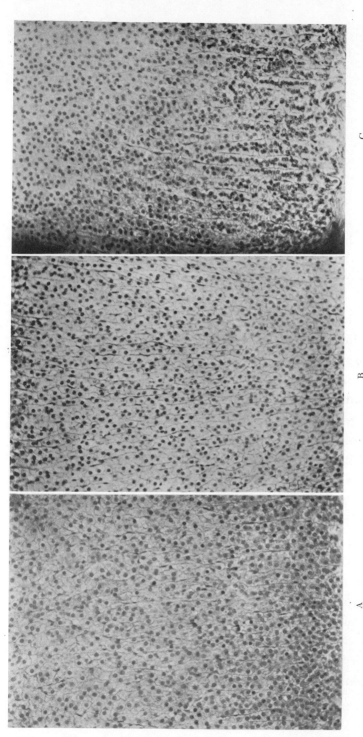

A

Section of Adrenal of Rabbit—Normal (× 310).

B

Section of Adrenal of Rabbit Showing Effect of Diphtheria Toxin (× 310).

Note the general disappearance of the cytoplasm.

C

Section of Adrenal of Rabbit Showing Effect of Diphtheria Toxin *Plus Morphin* (× 310).

Note the general presence and even distribution of cytoplasm in contrast with its disappearance in B.

Adrenals of rabbit—normal—diphtheria toxin—diphtheria toxin plus morphin.

FIG. 73.

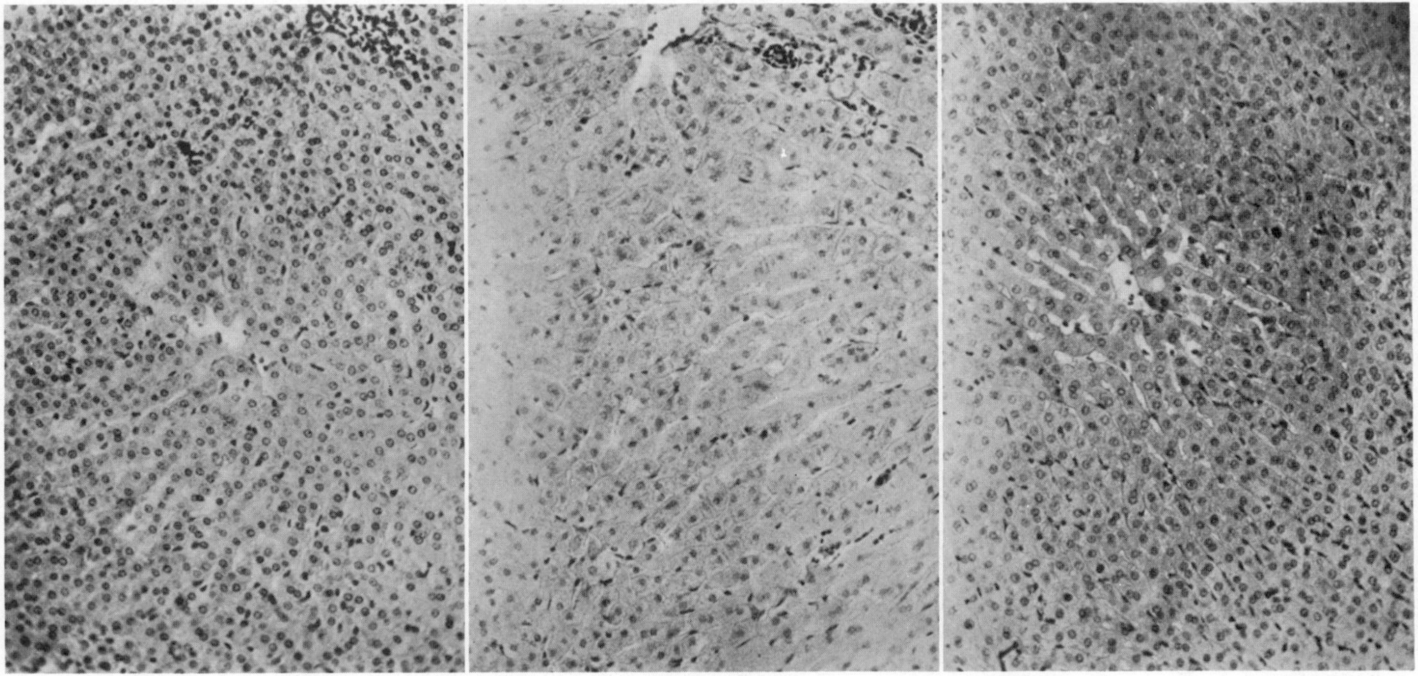

A

SECTION OF LIVER OF RABBIT—NORMAL
(× 310).

B

SECTION OF LIVER OF RABBIT SHOWING
EFFECT OF DIPHTHERIA TOXIN (× 310).

Note the poorly stained cells, their irregular outlines, the vacuolated spaces, and loss of cytoplasm.

C

SECTION OF LIVER OF RABBIT SHOWING
EFFECT OF DIPHTHERIA TOXIN *Plus Morphin* (× 310).

Note the regular arrangement of the cells and the even distribution of cytoplasm in contrast with the general disorganized condition of the cells in "B."

223

This conception of the kinetic system has stood a crucial test by making possible the shockless operation. It has offered a plausible explanation of the cause and the treatment of Graves' disease. Will the kinetic theory stand also the clinical test of controlling that protean disease bred in the midst of the stress of our present-day life? Present-day life, in which one must ever have one hand on the sword and the other on the throttle, is a constant stimulus of the kinetic system. The force of these kinetic stimuli may be lessened at the cerebral link by intelligent control—a protective control is empirically attained by many of the most successful men. The force of the kinetic stimuli may be broken at the thyroid link by dividing the nerve supply, reducing the blood supply, or by partial excision; or if the adrenals feel the strain, the stimulating force may be broken by dividing their nerve supply, reducing the blood supply, or by partial excision. No theory is worth more than its yield in practice, but already we have the shockless operation, the surgical treatment of Graves' disease, and the control of shock and of the acute infections by overwhelming morphinization (Figs. 62, 72, and 73).

Conclusions

To become adapted to their environment animals are transformers of energy. This adaptation to environment is made by means of a system of organs evolved for the purpose of converting potential energy into heat and motion. The principal organs and tissues of this system are the brain, the adrenals, the thyroid, the muscles, and the liver. Each is a vital link, each plays its particular rôle, and one cannot compensate for the other. A change in any link of the kinetic chain modifies proportionately the entire kinetic system which is no stronger than its weakest link.

In this conception we find a possible explanation of many diseases one which may point the way to new and more effective therapeutic measures than those now at our command.

ALKALESCENCE, ACIDITY, ANESTHESIA—A THEORY OF ANESTHESIA*

Alkalis and bases compose the greater part of the food of man and animals, the blood in both man and animals under normal conditions being slightly alkaline or rather potentially alkaline; that is, although in circulating blood the concentration of the OH-ions—upon which the degree of alkalinity depends— is but little more than in distilled water, yet blood has the power of neutralizing a considerable amount of acid (Starling, Wells). At the time of death, whatever its cause, the concentration of H-ions in the blood increases,—the concentration of H-ions being a measure of acidity,—that is, the potential or actual alkalinity decreases and the blood becomes actually neutral or acid.

To determine what conditions tend to diminish the normal alkalinity of the blood, many observations were made for me in my laboratory by Dr. M. L. Menten to determine by electric measurements the H-ion concentration of the blood under certain pathologic and physiologic conditions.

As a result of these researches we are able to state that the H-ion concentration of the blood—its acidity—is increased by excessive muscular activity; excessive emotional excitation; surgical shock; in the late stages of infection; by asphyxia; by strychnin convulsions; by inhalation anes-

* Paper delivered before the Virginia Medical Association, Washington, D. C., October 29, 1914.

227

thetics; after excision of the pancreas, and in the late stages of life after excision of the liver and excision of the adrenals. Morphin and decapitation cause no change in the H-ion concentration. Ether, nitrous oxid, and alcohol produce an increased acidity of the blood which is proportional to the depth of anesthesia.

Many of the cases studied were near death, as would be expected, since it is well known that a certain degree of acidity is incompatible with life.

Since alkalis and bases preponderate in ingested food; since alkalinity of the blood is diminished by bodily activity; and since at the point of death the blood is always acid, we may infer that some mechanism or mechanisms of the body were evolved for the purpose of changing bases into acids that thus energy might be liberated.

These observations lead naturally to the question, May not acidity of itself be the actual final cause of death? We believe that it may be so from the facts that—(1) The intravenous injection of certain acids causes death quickly, but that convulsions do not occur, since the voluntary muscles lose their power of contraction; and (2) the intravenous injection of acids causes extensive histologic changes in the brain, the adrenals, and the liver which resemble the changes invariably caused by activation of the kinetic system (Figs. 74 and 75). In view of these facts may we not find that anesthesia and many instances of unconsciousness are merely phenomena of acidity?

As has been stated already, we have found that the H-ion concentration of the blood—its acidity—is increased by alcohol, by ether, and by nitrous oxid. In addition our tests have shown that under ether the increase of the H-ion

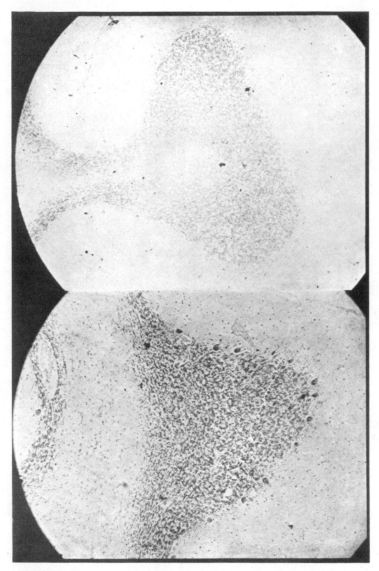

Fig. 74.

A

Section of Human Cerebellum—Normal (× 85).   Section of Human Cerebellum Showing the Effect of Acidosis (× 85).

B

Compare the faint traces of the Purkinje cells in B with the well-formed and distinct cells in A.

FIG. 75.

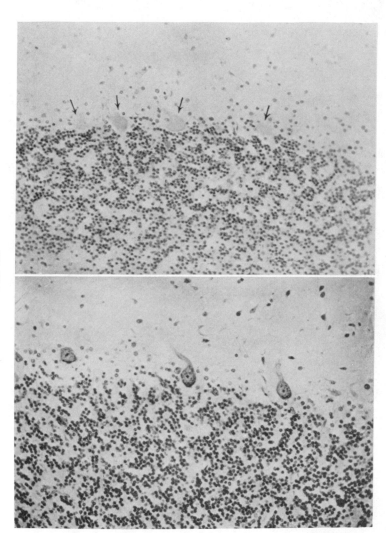

A

Section of Human Cerebellum—Normal (× 310).

B

Section of Human Cerebellum Showing the Effect of Acidosis (× 310).
There are no active cells present, and the Purkinje cells are but faintly visible (see arrows).

HUMAN CEREBELLUM—NORMAL AND ACIDOSIS

concentration—acidity—is more gradual than under nitrous oxid, an observation which accords well with the fact that nitrous oxid more quickly induces anesthesia than does ether.

Further striking testimony in favor of the hypothesis that the production of acidity by inhalation anesthetics is the method by which anesthesia itself is produced is found in the fact that although lethal doses of acid cause muscular paralysis, yet this paralysis may be mitigated by adrenalin—which is alkaline.   This observation may explain in part the remarkable success of the method of resuscitation devised by me, in which animals "killed" by anesthetics and asphyxia are revived by the use of adrenalin.

In animals under inhalation anesthesia Williams found that no nerve-current could be detected by the Einthoven string galvanometer, a fact which might be explained by postulating that nerve-currents can flow from the brain to the muscles and glands only when there is a difference of potential.   Any variation from the normal alkalinity of the body must change the difference in potential.   Since the nerve-currents in animals under anesthesia are not demonstrable by any apparatus at our command, and since anesthesia produces acidity, then we may infer that acidity reduces the difference in potential.   As long as there is life, a galvanometer of sufficient delicacy would perforce detect a nerve-current until the acidity increased to such a point as to reduce the difference in potential to zero—the point of death.   If at this point a suitable alkali—adrenalin solution —can be introduced quickly enough, the vital difference in potential may be restored and the life processes will be renewed.   Bearing especially on this point is the fact that if adrenalin in sufficient quantities be administered simultaneously with an acid, it will not only prevent the fall in blood-pressure usually caused by the acid, but will also prevent the histologic changes in the brain, adrenals, and liver which are usually caused by the intravenous injection of acids.

This hypothesis regarding the cause of anesthesia and unconsciousness explains and harmonizes many facts. It explains how asphyxia, overwhelming emotion, and excessive muscular exertion, by causing acidity, may produce unconsciousness. It explains the acidosis which results from starvation, from uremia, from diabetes, from Bright's disease, and supplies a reason for the use of intravenous infusions of sodium bicarbonate to overcome the coma of diabetes and uremia (Fig. 76). It may explain the quick death from chloroform and nitrous oxid; and may perhaps show why unconsciousness is so commonly the immediate precursor of death.

One of the most noticeable immediate effects of the administration of an inhalation anesthetic is a marked increase in the rapidity and force of the respiration. The respiratory center has evidently been evolved to act with an increase of vigor which is proportional—within certain limits—to the increase in the H-ion concentration, whereas the centers governing the voluntary muscles are inhibited. In this antithetic reaction of the higher cortical centers and the lower centers in the medulla to acidity we find a remarkable adaptation which prevents the animal from killing itself by the further increase in acidity which would be produced by muscular activity. That is, as the acidity produced by muscular action increases and threatens life, the respiratory action, by which carbon dioxid is eliminated and oxygen

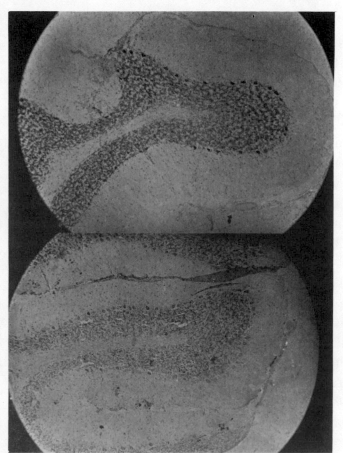

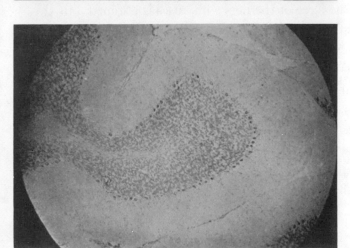

233

A.—Section of Cerebellum of Cat—Normal (× 85).

B.—Section of Cerebellum of Cat showing Effect of Injections of Leucin and Creatin.

Compare the general destructive effect of these acids with the protective effect of alkalies as in "C."

C.—Section of Cerebellum of Cat showing Effect of Injections of Sodium Bicarbonate.

The protective effect of the alkali is strikingly shown by the general hyperchromatism. Compare with effect of acid shown in "B."

supplied, is increased, while the driving power of the brain, which produces acidity, is diminished or even inhibited entirely; that is, the state of unconsciousness or anesthesia is reached. We conclude first that, without this life-saving regulation, animals under stress would inevitably commit suicide; and, second, that it is probable that the remarkable phenomenon of anesthesia—the coincident existence of un-consciousness and life—is due to this antithetic action of the cortex and the medulla.

In the human, as in the animal, the degree of acidity parallels the depth of inhalation anesthesia.

Within a few seconds after beginning nitrous oxid anes-thesia the acidity of the blood is increased. This rapid acidulation is synchronous with almost instantaneous un-consciousness and increased respiration. If the oxygen in the inhaled mixture be increased, a decrease in acidity is again synchronous with lighter anesthesia and a decrease in the respiratory rate.

If these premises be sound, we are justified in asserting that the state of anesthesia is due to an induced acidity of the blood. If the acidity is slight, then the anesthesia is slight and the force of the nerve impulses is lessened, but the patient is still conscious of them. As the acidity increases associative memory is lost, and the patient is said to be unconscious: the centers governing the voluntary muscles are not inhibited, however, and cutting the skin causes movements. If the acidity is further increased, there is loss of muscular tone and even the strong contact ceptor stimuli of a surgical operation do not cause any muscular response, and, finally, the acidity may be increased to the point at which the respiratory and circulatory centers can no longer respond by increased effort, and anesthetic death—that is, *acid* death—follows.

Certain clinical phenomena are clarified by this theory and serve to substantiate it. For example, it is well known that inhalation anesthesia precipitates the impending acidosis which results from starvation, from extreme Graves' disease, from great exhaustion, from surgical shock, and from hemorrhage, and which is present when death from any cause is imminent.

We see, therefore, that anesthesia is made possible, first, by the fact that inhalation anesthetics cause acidity, and, second, by the antithetic adaptation of the higher centers in the brain and of the centers governing respiration and circulation.

In deep contrast to the action of inhalation anesthetics is that of narcotics. Deep narcotization with morphin and scopolamin is induced slowly; the respiratory and pulse-rate are progressively lessened—and there is no acidity.

By our researches we have established in what consists the generic difference between inhalation anesthetics and narcotics. In our experiments no increase in the H-ion concentration was produced by morphin or by scopolamin, no matter how deep the narcotization. In animals already narcotized by morphin the production of acid by any of the acid-producing stimuli was delayed or prevented. On the other hand, in animals in which an acidity had already been produced by ether, by shock, by anger, or by fear, the later administration of morphin delayed or inhibited entirely the neutralization of the acidity. In other words, morphin interferes with the normal mechanism by which acidity is neutralized possibly because its inhibiting action on the respiratory center is sufficient to overcome the stimulating action of acidity on that center, for, as we have stated, the neutralization of acidity is in large measure accomplished by the increased respiration induced by the acidity itself.

SUMMARY

Acidity inhibits the functions of the cerebral cortex, but stimulates those of the medulla. This antithetic reaction to the stimulus of increased H-ion concentration is an adaptation to prevent animals from committing suicide by overactivity, for the mechanism for the initiation and control of the transformation of energy is in the higher centers of the brain, while an essential part of the mechanism for the neutralization of acidity—the centers governing circulation and respiration—is in the medulla. This explains many clinical phenomena—why excessive acidity causes paralysis; why there is great thirst after inhalation anesthesia, after excessive muscular activity, excessive emotion—after all those activities which we have found to be acid-producing, for water, like air, neutralizes acids. The excessive use of alcohol, anesthetics, excessive work, intense emotion, all produce lesions of the kidney and of the liver. The explanation is found in the fact that all these stimuli increase the acidity of the blood, and that, if long continued, the neutralizing mechanism must be broken down and so the end-products of metabolism are insufficiently prepared for elimination.

In view of these considerations we may well conclude that the maintenance of the normal potential alkalinity of the blood is to be estimated as the keystone of the foundation of life itself.

INDEX

237

DATE DUE

FEB 0 1 1996			